W9-CGN-693

Publications of the

CENTER FOR EDUCATION IN AFRICA
INSTITUTE OF INTERNATIONAL STUDIES

TEACHERS COLLEGE, COLUMBIA UNIVERSITY

James R. Sheffield and David G. Scanlon, editors

EDITORIAL BOARD

Nicholas O. Anim, Head
Department of Education
University College of Cape Coast
Cape Coast, Ghana

John Cameron, Lecturer
Department of Education in Tropical
Areas
Institute of Education
University of London

Babs Fafunwa, Dean
Faculty of Education
University of Ife
Ile-Ife, Nigeria

Mulugeta Wodajo, Academic
Vice President
Haile Selassie I University
Addis Ababa, Ethiopia

Senteza Kajubi, Director
National Institute of Education
Makerere University
Kampala, Uganda

STUDYING SCHOOL CHILDREN IN UGANDA:
FOUR REPORTS OF EXPLORATORY RESEARCH
Millie Almy, Joel R. Davitz, and Mary Alice White

CULTURAL ADAPTATION WITHIN MODERN AFRICA
S. H. Irvine and J. T. Sanders, Editors

THE DEVELOPMENT OF OPERATIONAL THINKING
IN PRIMARY SCHOOL CHILDREN
Barnabas Otaala

EDUCATION IN KENYA: AN HISTORICAL STUDY
James R. Sheffield

Education in Kenya:
An Historical Study

JAMES R. SHEFFIELD

Center for Education in Africa
Institute of International Studies
Teachers College, Columbia University

TEACHERS COLLEGE PRESS
Teachers College, Columbia University
New York and London

0354624   73001

© 1973 by Teachers College, Columbia University
Library of Congress Catalog Card Number: 72-88639

Manufactured in the United States of America

Preface

In this study, Professor Sheffield analyzes the development of education in Kenya within the broader framework of the society at large. *Education in Kenya,* one of the first historical studies of the subject, traces the role of education from traditional society through the colonial period to the post-Independence period. The study examines the various policies as they emerged in response to changing needs, and points to the difficulties of implementing these policies.

Professor Sheffield has been particularly close to educational developments in Kenya, having served as an advisor in the Kenya Ministry of Education under the auspices of the Ford Foundation from 1965 to 1967. Among his other publications, Professor Sheffield was the editor of *Education, Employment and Rural Development,* the report of the influential Kericho Conference, and the author of *Education in the Republic of Kenya.*

D.G.S.

Introduction

The ways in which any society educates its younger members are determined by a complex set of forces beyond the control of educators. This study analyzes the development of Kenya's formal school system within the framework of the broader society. Rather than simply describing what the educational system was like, it focuses on the policy issues that shaped the system. Policy has often been seen from the narrow view of what is stated in official documents or reports. Although this study deals with most of the major official documents of the British colonial government and independent Kenya, as well as with international conferences, a particular effort has also been made to consider the role of the people affected by the policies in influencing the formulation of those policies.

Increasingly, historical studies have recognized the importance of African initiatives. Historians of the colonial period, for example, no longer simply attribute major changes to the actions of the colonial regimes upon a passive African population; while immigrant groups—European and Asian—played an important part in Kenya's development, this book concentrates primarily on the education of the African population. Since Kenya achieved independence in December, 1963, there have been significant developments and new interpretations of the colonial experience.

The following study is a much-revised version of a doctoral dissertation completed at Teachers College, Columbia University, in 1964. After working on a survey of manpower needs and educational capabilities in Africa during 1964-65, I worked in the Kenya Ministry of Education from 1965-67, under the auspices of the Ford Foundation. It was a great privilege to be involved in the formative stages of so many important educational developments, and it gave me an opportunity to gather new data and to update and revise the dissertation.

I am greatly indebted to my former colleagues in the Ministry of Education for their patience and help in my work. In revising my earlier manuscript Peter H. Lary, Albert H. Barclay, Jr., and Clifford Gilpin provided expert assistance in research and rewriting.

6

Contents

0354624

73001

SUDAN

ETHIOPIA

*Lake
Rudolf*

UGANDA

KENYA

SOMALI REPUBLIC

White highlands
settlement area

●Kericho

*Lake
Victoria*

●Nairobi

AFRICA

KENYA

INDIAN

OCEAN

Mombasa

TANZANIA

CHAPTER I

The Foundations of Education in Kenya

TRADITIONAL SOCIETY AND EDUCATION

In his now famous book on the Kikuyu, *Facing Mount Kenya,* Jomo Kenyatta wrote, "Education begins at the time of birth and ends with death (1)." The common conception of education as that which takes place in schools fails to consider the wide variety of teaching and learning that goes on outside any formal institution. In any society, the preparation of people both young and old for the tasks they will encounter later in life is done by a combination of formal and informal means. Although throughout this study the word education refers mainly to the formal school system, the absence of such institutions in traditional cultures makes such a distinction somewhat arbitrary.

Traditional education cannot be separated from society, because both are interwoven within the same cultural fabric. Although both formal and informal methods were used, education was much more closely integrated into the daily life of the individual in various East African tribes than in modern societies (2). There were no buildings or organizations comparable to modern schools, nor was teaching a distinct profession. There was considerable educational activity, however, which occurred in more concentrated form at certain times than at others, for example, during the initiation of a group of youths into adulthood. As a whole, traditional education was not specialized or institutionalized to the extent that education is in modern societies (3).

An important characteristic of traditional societies was their inability to control the natural environment to the degree that modern societies, with their advanced technology, can. The vulnerability of Kenya's traditional societies was increased by their poverty and cultural isolation. With subsistence agriculture the predominant economic activity, life was constantly on the edge of calamity. In the face of adversity, and in the absence of advanced technology, the best weapons were social cohesiveness and communal responsibility. Thus, traditional education had to be geared to fostering and preserving these values, rather than imparting knowledge and skills oriented toward individual advancement.

Melville Herskovits had identified three ways in which the primarily social purpose of traditional education was achieved: informally, by parents and elders in the society; formally, by apprenticeship to craftsmen; and by initiation rites (4).

The early education of the African child took place in and around the home. It took the form of games, riddles, stories, and specific instructions concerning the correct behavior to adopt towards his numerous relatives and other members of the community. The kinship knowledge thus acquired was particularly important, because position in the clan and lineage was an important determinant of status and privileges. Traditional education was concerned "with personal relations, rather than with natural phenomena (5)." Nevertheless, natural phenomena and practical knowledge were also imparted, largely in the course of participating in the work of the home and farm. Science was not taught as an abstract and unified body of knowledge, as it is in modern education; the traditional method was "to teach the names of particular plants, the use of different trees, or the management of a particular herd of sheep and goats or cattle (6)."

Traditional education also provided individuals with the opportunity to acquire specialized skills as wood-carvers, tanners, blacksmiths, hunters, beekeepers, or medicine men. These occupations were in most cases hereditary, but even so the emphasis was on learning by practical application skills important to the maintenance of the society.

In essence, a tribesman's whole life was marked by his progress from one initiation to another, and hence from one level of social status to a higher one. As the child matured, he graduated to successively higher levels, and as an adult, gained further prestige when he was accepted among the elders, who commanded the greatest respect of all. The rites of passage from childhood to maturity stand out as the most important and dramatic of all these transitions. Whatever other formal and informal means were used, these rites usually culminated in an initiation ceremony, frequently associated with circumcision or other physical ordeals. This initiation was the outward sign that an individual was ready to assume the responsibilities of adulthood, and until it was complete, "no young man could be considered a full member of his society (7)."

After initiation, young men and women often underwent a period of recuperation and instruction outside their native communities. This "bush school" lasted from a few weeks to six or eight months in some cases. While the young people recovered from the physical ordeal of initiation, they were introduced to tribal lore and traditions. In Kenya, instruction did not usually include the specialized preparation for artistic, religious, or professional functions that took place in some African societies. Instead, the initiates were given the basic knowledge necessary to assure that the identity of the tribal community would persist from one generation to the next.

The initiation ceremony and subsequent period of isolation were often the first real opportunity for an individual to loosen the bonds which linked him as a child to his parents. Among the Kikuyu, all youths who were circumcised at a given time constituted an exclusive lifelong fraternity called an age-set, or age group. This group was the first forum in which young adults could gain political experience and demonstrate their leadership, and through deeds of military prowess the group could acquire remarkable solidarity. In the words of Jomo Kenyatta:

The fellowship and unity of these age-groups is rather a remarkable thing. It binds men from all parts of the country, and though they may have been circumcized at places hundreds of miles apart, it is of no consequence (8).

As long as the tribal societies remained relatively isolated, traditional education served to perpetuate a stable system of social relations. However, the coming of the Europeans affected the entire fabric of traditional cultures. Even before modern education could have any impact, it became evident that the African population of Kenya would be the main source of labor for the new ruling class. The present-day economic, social, and political framework of Kenya is the result of 70 years of British dominance. The African societies were affected both internally and in their relations with outsiders by the new pattern imposed on them.

Traditional education could not prevent the often painful dislocation of tribal societies, nor could it meet the demands placed on them by the new order. Modern education, as alien to the tribes in form, content, and aims as the rest of the developing new culture was, became part of the new framework. And for a few—the ambitious, the privileged or, in many cases, the failures who couldn't make it in their own culture—modern education became a means of participating in the changes that were taking place. Nevertheless, the spirit and motivating force of traditional education survived, and in later years were to reassert themselves continuously. Gradually, it was recognized that modern education was contributing to the decay of tribal culture. A demand arose for a new educational system, Western in form and much of its content, but aimed at preserving vital elements of the old society.

Many aspects of traditional education still remain, marking the passage from childhood into adult society, and training the many children who receive little or no formal schooling. But, as a result of the westernization, and especially urbanization, to which the culture was exposed, traditional institutions and their powerful sanctions have broken down, leaving many Africans caught between two worlds.

BEGINNINGS OF COLONIZATION

British influence was supreme along the coasts of eastern Africa from the time of the Napoleonic Wars until the mid-1960's. Britain's early interest in the area was mainly strategic—to cover the flank of the ocean route to India, while maintaining a proper political environment for the commercial activities of her Indian subjects. The Sultan of Zanzibar served as the ready-made instrument of Britain's strategic requirements; the thriving commercial empire created by Seyyid Said and his successors was no financial burden to Britain, yet was vulnerable enough to a judicious use of naval power and diplomacy to constitute a pliable ally. It was so pliable, in fact, that the Sultan, contrary to his economic and political self-interest, as well as to the Muslim ethic, was expected to be "the Wilberforce of East Africa and lead the fight against the slave trade (9)." As restriction of the trade became more rigid, it became necessary to replace mere influence exerted from outside with "barely disguised informal control" exerted by the British Consul in Zanzibar (10). But the official mood of Britain was against territorial commitments, and it was only with great reluctance that informal control was converted into formal control in the last decade of the nineteenth century.

By the time Zanzibar became a protectorate in 1890, new factors were at work and had already deprived the Sultan of the better part of his mainland sphere of influence. German claims in Tanganyika were defined in Anglo-German treaties in 1886 and 1890, thus establishing a new imperial power astride Zanzibar's main trade routes to the interior. Catholic (French), Protestant (English), and Muslim (Arab) factions were warring for supremacy in the powerful state of Buganda. After the calamity of Gordon's death at Khartoum no British Government could entirely evade the obligation of supporting the efforts of the English missionaries. The British also felt that their continued presence in Egypt required control of the whole Nile Valley, including its source in Uganda, especially as there was evidence of a French advance towards the Nile from West Africa. Even so, Great Britain remained reluctant to assume responsibilities in East Africa. Instead, a chartered company, the Imperial British East Africa (IBEA) Company, was given the task of creating an effective presence and a semblance of order in that region. Captain Frederick Lugard was sent to Buganda in 1890 to place it under the Company's protection. Lugard obtained the grudging cooperation of the Kabaka (King) of Buganda, and was able to overcome the threat of the Catholic faction which, largely because the presence of the IBEA Company enhanced the prestige of the Protestant group, opposed the Company's influence. However, the Company was not equipped to maintain stability in the area. It struggled on the brink of bankruptcy until 1893, when the British Government had to intervene. In 1894, Britain declared a formal protectorate in Uganda. The following year, the rest of the British sphere of influence, including the area between Uganda and the ocean, was designated as the East African Protectorate (EAP).

Until 1900, the EAP, a substantial portion of present-day Kenya, "was looked upon as little more than a supply route to Uganda (11)." Uganda, with its established kingdoms and highly developed societies, was considered an ideal setting for missionaries, while Kenya was considered too wild and inhospitable. Hence, its administration was simply annexed to the responsibilities of the British agent at Zanzibar. But there were already developments that would have a profound effect on the status and character of Kenya as a colonial society. The spearhead of these new developments was the construction of the Uganda Railway, from 1895 to 1901, which provided an effective link from the coast to Lake Victoria, and strengthened British control of the Nile headwaters. The mere presence of the railway would have had a significant impact on the African societies of Kenya, but its revolutionary effects were multiplied by creating conditions under which the dream of white settlement could become a reality. British spokesmen considered white settlement necessary in order to make the protectorate a going concern and obtain some return on the considerable outlay for the construction of the railroad. With the active encouragement of the Protectorate Commissioner, Charles Eliot, "settlers began to arrive in numbers in 1903," many of them from South Africa (12).

The construction of the railway also led to the arrival of what became Kenya's largest immigrant community. Thousands of laborers were imported from India to work on the railway, and thousands more Asians followed, until at Independence there were nearly 200,000 Asians in Kenya, completely dominating the commercial sector of the economy.

THE FORMATION OF A COLONIAL POLICY

When Great Britain assumed responsibility for the East African Protectorate in 1895, her primary goal was to keep the line of communication to Uganda open. This goal had expanded by 1902, when the completion of the railroad and the addition of a large area in the highlands pointed to the possibility of developing a settler economy in the territory. The decision to encourage European settlement was also affected by Britain's insistence that its colonies pay for themselves (13). In some parts of Africa, such as the Niger delta, there was already an established export trade that could be taxed to support the colonial administration. In others, like Uganda, conditions were suitable for the development of commercial peasant agriculture. For various reasons, these possibilities did not exist in Kenya, where political and commercial sophistication had not evolved to a comparable degree, and where vast expanses of land which appeared underused and underpopulated attracted prospective European settlers.

It is interesting to note that while Frederick Jackson, the Acting Commissioner, encouraged Asian farmers both in Kenya and in India about the prospects of obtaining land (14), Eliot, who succeeded him as Commissioner, wanted to avoid any competition between immigrant races in the highlands (15), and therefore came to the conclusion that Kenya should be a "white man's country." Eliot's view was confirmed in 1906 by the Secretary of State for the Colonies, Lord Elgin. Although Winston Churchill, the Under-Secretary, was able to modify this view slightly, the highlands remained essentially reserved for Europeans (16).

The East African Order in Council of 1901 "attempted to place the alienation of land to Europeans on a sound basis by laying down that any land alienated must be Crown land, that is, land not already occupied by Africans (17)." It appears that the British Government was sincere in its efforts to recognize African claims, but the overworked Land Office was unable to investigate African claims or survey the land properly. By 1904, the Land Office was besieged by an impatient flood of settlers, and in its haste to accommodate them, a great deal of land north of Nairobi was alienated. This was a zone which had recently been occupied by the Kikuyu, whose population had been drastically reduced by several national disasters in the late nineteenth century; they would eventually have reclaimed it.

Friction over the demarcation of African lands was to become a potent stimulus to the development of African political consciousness in later years. Although a half century of settler occupation, perpetuating the disparity between overcrowded African reserves and the broad expanses of the white highlands, eventually triggered a major political crisis, originally the conflict regarding land distribution was only one aspect of the basic incompatibility between the native peasant societies and the powerful alien minority in their midst. The seven percent of Kenya's land alienated to the settlers seems a relatively minor portion at first, considering that 49 percent and 87 percent were taken by European settlers in Rhodesia and South Africa respectively. But this seven percent included over one-fifth of all available agricultural land with high potential for successful cultivation, and the settlers occupying this land made up less than one percent of Kenya's total population.

The fundamental importance of land in traditional societies dependent upon subsistence agriculture further complicated the land issue in Kenya. It was and is difficult for people accustomed to industrialized societies to grasp the almost mystical reverence for land that is characteristic in African communities. Anthropologists have consistently noted and stressed the significance of the earth as the home of ancestral spirits and the source of all life. Jomo Kenyatta was one of the early and most articulate spokesmen for his tribe, the Kikuyu, who were so deeply affected by colonial land policies. Throughout *Facing Mount Kenya,* Kenyatta stresses the vital importance of land, describing the Crown Lands scheme as "insidious trickery" by which the Kikuyu "lost most of their lands through their magnanimity . . . [becoming] tenants at the will of the Crown (18)." Kenyatta goes on to say that when the European takes tribal lands "he is taking away not only their livelihood, but the national symbol that holds family and tribe together. In doing this he gives one blow which cuts away the foundations from the whole of Gikuyu [Kikuyu] life, social, moral, and economic (19)."

Although the Kikuyu bore the brunt of the direct effects of land alienation, no tribe was unaffected by the Government's land policy. In limiting the grazing grounds of the Masai, a nomadic, warlike tribe, an unfortunate precedent was set in 1905 and 1906 which, it appeared, "would at all times favour the claims of European settlers at the expense of the needs of the African population. . . . For occupied as well as unoccupied land within the [African] reserves might still be alienated if the Governor obtained the consent of the Secretary of State (20)." The Government's ignorance and inefficient handling of the claims, combined with the scheming of Lord Delamere, the settlers' champion, resulted in an injustice (21). The division of land among the various races and tribes created a legacy of ill-feeling that was to remain with the territory for many years.

The crux of Kenya's colonial situation was that the settlers could not make a success of their farming merely by living alongside the Africans, as if they were just another tribe competing for the scarce land. To prosper, they needed labor, and to secure a labor force, they had to strengthen their hold over the African population. The means for forcing Africans to work for wages were already available in the form of the hut tax, which from 1901 on was imposed on each area as it came under administrative control (22). Taxation might, in some cases, have been a spur to development of peasant agriculture, but in Kenya, Africans were forbidden to grow cash crops such as coffee or tea. The only alternative method of raising cash to pay taxes was working for the Europeans. During the early twentieth century, settlers constantly applied pressure on the Government to increase the supply of cheap labor for their isolated farms (23). In 1905, when control of the territory was transferred from the Foreign Office to the Colonial Office, a primary task of the Governor, Sir James Sadler, was to set up an appointive Legislative Council. One of the settlers' most vocal spokesmen, Lord Delamere, was appointed to the Council, and by 1911, the settlers' interests were represented by numerous local associations. In order to coordinate their efforts, a Convention of Associations, or "Settlers' Parliament" as it was known, was formed with the principal purpose of achieving elected representation in the Legislative Council (24). Although this goal was not attained until 1919, a significant trend was established. The Government's early decision to develop a settler economy boomeranged in a sense, as the settlers demanded an increased role in running the Government, while the Colonial Office in principle protected the interests of the Africans.

By 1920, the settlers' demands were the principal consideration in the formulation of land and labor policy. A sizable area was excised from the Nandi reserve as a settlement scheme for World War I veterans, and Government officials were exhorted by settlers' circulars to help in recruiting labor (25). This was tantamount to legitimizing compulsory labor, however, and there was strong protest from interests that were not committed to the settler cause. The missions played an important role at this time by lobbying in behalf of African interests in London. In 1921, the Reverend J. H. Oldham of the International Missionary Council sent a private memorandum to the Colonial Office protesting Governor Northey's inclination toward establishment of a system of compulsory labor in Kenya, and citing the harmful effect on Africans of leaving them no choice but to work on European-owned farms; he urged that the Government pursue a policy to "maintain tribal life . . . and to develop by education the industry and intelligence of the population (26)." In the same year, Colonial Secretary Winston Churchill, who had visited Kenya in 1907 and come away unconvinced that its future was as a "white man's country," sent a dispatch to officials in Kenya instructing them merely to give out job information and prohibiting them from taking part in labor recruiting.

From the early years of British rule in Kenya, there was a fundamental contradiction between the aspirations of the settlers to transplant British parliamentary tradition and their determination to solidify their position as a colonial elite. Guy Hunter explains the contradiction in terms of "the European dream of political and social segregation within a single economy," dominated by the settlers (27). It is in this ambivalent situation that the foundations of modern education were laid in Kenya.

EDUCATION BY THE MISSIONS

Within this framework of racial segregation and European domination, the missions enjoyed a virtual monopoly in the field of African education until the 1920's. Even after it had assumed primary responsibility for African education after World War II, the Government continued to support the role of the missions as another arm of European administrative influence.

Missionaries were active in what is now Kenya some 50 years before the British Government assumed responsibility for the territory. Johann Krapf established a mission station at Rabai, near Mombasa, in 1844 for the Anglican Church Missionary Society (CMS). However, the coastal tribes were not particularly receptive to the severe pietism of this CMS pioneer, in many ways antithetical to the relaxed style of the Wanyika tribes of the coast. Twenty years after the foundation of the mission at Rabai, a visitor found a mere "six baptised converts with another six under tuition (28)." Nor was Krapf's project of starting "a mission-chain between East and West Africa" ever launched (29). Krapf had a discouraging experience with the difficulties of access to the interior highlands, and nearly lost his life when the party of Kamba travelers he was with was ambushed near Embu country east of Mt. Kenya. It was in part because of the dangers of travel that the area between the Kenya coast and Lake Victoria remained free of missionary penetration until after government protection and the railroad had appeared.

This pattern contrasted with Tanganyika and Uganda where, in more typical sequence, the flag followed the Bible.

The pietism of the first CMS mission at Mombasa, with its emphasis on conversion and scripture, was too barren of results to satisfy the increasing missionary energy manifested later in the nineteenth century. David Livingstone, whose epic career had aroused British public opinion to the "great social evils of African society," had argued that the primary task of missions was to spread Christian (i.e., Western) civilization and supplant the slave trade by legitimate commerce, and that only in this way could the foundations for meaningful conversions be laid (30). Although Livingstone's plan to establish centers of Christian civilization from which the economic and spiritual transformation of African society could be effected met with initial failure, his strategy of combining social change with evangelization found ready application in slightly modified form.

By the 1870's, Britain's mounting campaign against the slave trade led to the recovery of close to 1,000 slaves each year. The question of the disposal of these forcibly detribalized persons was solved by handing them over to the missions. Of these, the Catholic mission at Bagamoyo, on the Tanganyika coast opposite Zanzibar, was especially successful in the creation of large self-sustaining communities of former slaves. Sir Bartle Frere, who negotiated the total abolition of the seaborne slave trade with Sultan Barghash in 1873, was so impressed that he recommended Bagamoyo as a model for the CMS to follow. This resulted in the foundation of Freretown outside Mombasa in 1875. It was to become the largest freed slave settlement of its kind in East Africa (31). The later work of the original stations near Mombasa as well was determined by the special conditions arising from the intensified abolition movement at the end of the nineteenth century. Following Freretown's example, the care of freed or escaped slaves became the chief preoccupation of the mission at Rabai, replacing its disheartening attempts to proselytize the worldly Wanyika.

Nevertheless, the educational work of the CMS missions continued, and foreshadowed some of the main dichotomies of education in the twentieth century. Under Krapf and his early successors, education at Rabai was intellectual in orientation if not in content. It sought to inculcate basic literacy, for reading Scripture, and manual tasks were chiefly valued for their supposed moral benefits. At Freretown, and later at Rabai, however, the missionaries' goal was to create model self-sustaining communities—hence education was practical and aimed at production. Thus, both lines of educational thinking, ranging from advocacy of abstract training of the mind to a commitment to rudimentary agricultural training, were already present in the mission origins of formal education in Kenya. Individualism, competition, and elitism were in a sense foreshadowed at Rabai by Krapf and his associates, while the creation of self-reliant communities, such as at Freretown, was a reality long before it became a controversial doctrine.

The Missions and the Empire

Many British observers saw the missions as a means of furthering the colonial cause. Sir Harry Johnston, who claimed to have first suggested the Cape-to-Cairo idea to Cecil Rhodes in 1889, advocated the use of missionaries as the advance guard of an expanding British empire:

The missionary is really gaining your experience for you without any cost to yourself. . . . . They strengthen our hold over the country, they spread the use of the English language, they induct the natives into the best kind of civilization, and in fact, each mission station is an essay in colonization (32).

The British Government was generally favorably disposed towards the activities of the missions. Roland Oliver noted the tendency of mission stations to become "a power in the land and not a spiritual power only (33)." The initial advantage of the missionary presence to the Government was its contribution to the "softening" of traditional societies, which removed impediments to the extension of administration. But the missions soon performed another essential service by training "interpreters and policemen . . . builders and joiners . . . messengers, orderlies and domestic servants (34)." Thus, almost from the beginning, educational activities grew to be their major contribution to the colonial society, and their expansion welcomed by the Government.

After the establishment of the British East African Protectorate in 1895 and the completion of the railway to Kisumu in 1901, the missionary occupation of the central highlands and the shores of Lake Victoria was extremely rapid. In 1894, apart from Rabai and Freretown, there was only one mission outpost among the Taita, and the Church of Scotland mission at Kibwezi established by the director of the Imperial British East Africa Company. The latter mission was transferred to Kikuyu, near Nairobi, in 1898. The Anglican Church Missionary Society also established itself in the Kikuyu country in 1901 at Kihuruko. New posts were opened at Weithega (1903), Kahuhia (1906), Mahiga (1908), and Embu (1910). The Catholics opened their drive into Kikuyu country at Kiambu (1902), followed by Limuru (1903), and Mangu (1906). The fundamentalist Africa Inland Mission station at Kijabe was opened in 1901. Nyanza, the northeastern shores of Lake Victoria, was first penetrated from Uganda, since it was under Uganda administration until 1902.

Partly in recognition of the work of the missions, and in the process of assuming some responsibility for education, the Government established a Department of Education in 1911 and made financial grants for every pupil who passed an exam set up by one of the Government departments. Until that time the only help received by the missions had been in the form of land grants on which to establish themselves; in 1918 the grants were made contingent on Government inspection of the mission schools' training facilities.

A close relationship between the missions and Kenya's settlers was also developing in the years before World War I. This was reflected in the Kikuyu saying, *Gutiri mubea na muthunga,* which means, "There is no difference between a missionary and a settler (35)." A Kenyan scholar commented that mission schools "became closely linked with settlers' needs (36)." As the compulsory labor issue indicated, this had not always been the case, but more important than the historical accuracy of the saying was the fact that a significant group of Africans shared the sentiment. In the Africans' view, the missions, settlers, and Government were virtually inseparable aspects of the colonial establishment.

Summary

Although the details of the missions' educational efforts varied, it is possible to identify some general aspects of mission education. According to Oliver, the first goal of missionary education was to gain converts and train catechists who could both preach and teach, but literacy soon became a basic concern, since Protestants had to be able to read the Bible for baptism (37). In addition, most curricula were soon broadened to include manual training. The relative importance of religious instruction, literacy, and humanistic education on the one hand, and technical training on the other, was a constant source of disagreement in missionary circles. In reporting on the International Conference held at Le Zoute, Belgium, September 14-21, 1926, the Reverend Edwin Smith defined the goal of missionary education as "to fashion character after the pattern of Christ," by maintaining a religious basis in all subjects (38).

The missions differed widely in their interpretation of this goal, however, and at the Jeanes Conference in 1935, two speakers advocated divergent approaches to Christian education. The Reverend Dougall, who had spent many years in Kenya, stated that "in the history or reading lesson he [the Christian teacher] will be teaching history and reading, not religion . . . religion will pervade the teaching of non-religious subjects, but as an energy and inspiration, not as dogmatic truth (39)." In striking contrast to Dougall, the Reverend H. W. Murray from Southern Rhodesia stressed "the great value of the memorization of Bible passages (40)."

Since the impact of Western culture upon traditional societies inevitably caused certain dislocations and conflicts, the challenge to the missionaries was whether they could adapt Christianity to the African setting with a minimum of disturbance. Othieno clearly identified the problem: "The missionaries failed to differentiate Christian ethics from the European way of life. To them, becoming a Christian generally meant negation of the traditional African way of life (41)." As events in the 1920's and 1930's demonstrated, Western institutions had to be adapted to African needs. As early as 1912, one missionary author predicted "that the rising nationalism of Asia and Africa would destroy Christianity along with Western Imperialism unless the faith could be early established under indigenous leadership (42)." Oliver acknowledged that after the war African Christianity began to acquire a momentum of its own (43).

Both the Government, in establishing the Education Department in 1911, and the churches took steps to coordinate the missions' educational efforts. In 1913 the Church of Scotland Mission called a conference at Kikuyu to establish a federation of Protestant missions in the territory, and although no African had a voice in the proceedings, it was a significant effort to coordinate educational policy, and the efforts bore fruit after the war (44).

Despite the lack of centralized control over standards or policy, the missions laid the foundations for future educational development in Kenya. The fact that the Government relied so heavily upon the voluntary agencies, long after assuming major responsibility for the education of Africans, was an acknowledgement of the missions' substantial contribution.

Notes

1. Jomo Kenyatta, *Facing Mount Kenya* (New York: Vintage, 1962), p. 96.

2. E. B. Castle, *Growing Up in East Africa* (London: Oxford University Press, 1966), p. 40.

3. N. Antipa Othieno, *An Outline of History of Education in East Africa, 1844-1925* (Ed.D. project report, Teachers College, Columbia University, 1963), p. 13.

4. Melville Herskovits, *The Human Factor in Changing Africa* (New York: Knopf, 1962), p. 222.

5. Kenyatta, *op. cit.*, p. 102.

6. *Ibid.*, p. 117.

7. David G. Scanlon, "The Bush School," *Phi Delta Kappan*, XLI, no. 4 (January, 1960), 148.

8. Kenyatta, *op. cit.*, p. 112.

9. R. Robinson and J. Gallagher, *Africa and the Victorians* (New York: Doubleday, 1961), p. 43.

10. *Ibid.*, p. 47.

11. Kenneth Ingham, *A History of East Africa* (London: Longmans, 1962), p. 205.

12. George Bennett, *Kenya: A Political History: The Colonial Period* (Oxford University Press, 1963), p. 12.

13. Sir Andrew Cohen, *British Policy in Changing Africa* (Evanston: Northwestern University Press, 1959), p. 16.

14. W. Macgregor Ross, *Kenya From Within* (London: Allen and Unwin, 1927), p. 301.

15. Sir Charles Eliot, *The East African Protectorate* (London: Edward Arnold, 1905), pp. 178-179.

16. Ingham, *op. cit.,* p. 216.

17. *Ibid.,* p. 212.

18. Kenyatta, *op. cit.,* p. 47.

19. *Ibid.,* p. 305.

20. Ingham, *op. cit.,* p. 215.

21. East African Protectorate, *Correspondence Relating to the Masai* (London: O.H.M.S., Cd. 5584 of 1911).

22. Ingham, *op. cit.,* pp. 52-53.

23. One settler defined the ideal reserve as "a convenient recruiting ground for labour, a place from which the able-bodied go out to work, returning occasionally to rest and beget the next generation of labourers." Lord Oliver, *White Capital and Coloured Labour* (London: Hogarth Press, 1929), p. 214.

24. Elspeth Huxley, *White Man's Country* (London: Chatto and Windus, 1935), I, 210-212, 276-280.

25. Bennett, *Kenya: A Political History,* pp. 43-44.

26. Roland Oliver, *The Missionary Factor in East Africa* (London: Longmans, Green, 1952), pp. 255-256.

27. Guy Hunter, *New Societies in Tropical Africa* (London: Oxford University Press, 1962), p. 25; see also Andrew Cohen, p. 21.

28. R. Oliver, *op. cit.,* p. 6.

29. *Ibid.,* p. 6.

30. *Ibid.,* pp. 9-11.

31. *Ibid.,* pp. 19-25 *et passim.*

32. *Ibid.,* p. 128. See also Rene Maunier, *The Sociology of Colonies,* E. O. Lorimer, ed. and translator (London: Routledge and K. Paul, 1949), I, 23.

33. R. Oliver, *op. cit.,* p. 50.

34. *Ibid.,* p. 177.

35. F. B. Welbourn, *East Africa Rebels: A Study of Some Independent Churches* (London: S.C.M. Press, 1961), p. 111.

36. Othieno, *op. cit.,* p. 158.

37. R. Oliver, *op. cit.*, p. 213.

38. Edwin W. Smith, *The Christian Mission in Africa* (London: Edinburgh House Press, 1926), p. 109.

39. Carnegie Corporation of New York, *Village Education in Africa,* Report of the Inter-Territorial "Jeanes" Conference, Salisbury, Southern Rhodesia, May 27-June 6, 1935 (Lovedale, South Africa: Lovedale Press, 1935). Hereafter referred to as the Jeanes Conference.

40. *Ibid.*, p. 233.

41. Othieno, *op. cit.*, p. 22.

42. From *The Decision Hour of Christian Missions,* by John Mott (New York: 1912) quoted in Oliver, *op. cit.*, p. 233.

43. *Ibid.*, p. 229.

44. *Ibid.*, pp. 222-225.

CHAPTER II

Between the Wars

THE POLITICAL SETTING: DIVIDED INTERESTS

The political situation in Kenya between the world wars was marked by a growing tension resulting from two sets of circumstances. On the one hand, the economy was dominated by a settler minority striving to gain political control; on the other, Africans overwhelmingly outnumbered the immigrant population. Policy questions began increasingly to revolve around this fundamental dichotomy. By 1920 the Europeans had achieved elective representation in the Legislative Council, a step towards the settler-dominated "white man's country" they longed for. Although their aspirations were illusory, there was much in the post-World War I situation to encourage the settlers in their attempt to attain paramountcy: European settlers were nominated to the Executive Council; circulars issued by the strongly pro-settler Governor Northey gave District Officers considerable latitude in means of "encouraging" African labor to seek employment; the white highlands were considerably enlarged, a large area being excised from the Nandi reserve to allow for a Soldier Settlement scheme which was intended to double the European population; and Northey himself frequently stated that European interests must be paramount.

However, this trend met with unexpected resistance, which ultimately prevented Kenya from following Southern Rhodesia along the road to settler control (1). One source of opposition came from the first stirrings of political resistance on the part of the Africans. In 1921, Harry Thuku and the Young Kikuyu Association began to organize protests against the growing burdens imposed on the African population. As soon as the movement showed signs of extending itself from the politically aware Kikuyu to other tribes, it was suppressed by a combination of government action and missionary intervention. By interposing themselves between different tribes the missionaries were able to divert the political movements into what they considered moderate channels, arrogating to themselves the role of spokesmen for African interests.

A much more effective barrier to European ambitions at this time was the Indian community. Not only was it more than twice as large as the European population, but its strategic role in commerce and in urban real estate gave it considerable influence. It could also count on a degree of support from the powerful Indian Office in London, just as the white settlers looked to the South African Government for lobbying aid. The goal of the Asian population was to secure a guarantee of equal rights with the European population. But since this goal conflicted with the desire of the latter to perpetuate their supremacy, the whole issue of paramountcy of interests came to a head in the conflict between Europeans and Asians. In denying the possibility of Indian-elected representatives in the Legislative Council, the famous Devonshire White Paper of 1923, titled *Indians in Kenya,* crushed the European settlers' ambitions, and declared, "Primarily Kenya is an African territory . . . and that if and when those interests [the Africans'] and the interests of the immigrant races should conflict, the former should prevail (2)."

The doctrine of African paramountcy was reinforced in a further series of reports and actions by the British Government. The 1929 Hilton Young Report dealt principally with the question of "closer union" of Britain's territories in East and Central Africa, a union which would have increased settler influence by bringing Kenya closer to the orbit of the white supremacist territories. However, the report also affirmed that the correct relationship of the immigrant communities to the indigenous population was one of "partnership, not control (3)."

In 1931, the report of a parliamentary Joint Select Committee dismissed for the foreseeable future any hope of European-controlled responsible government (4). And in 1932, Lord Moyne conducted a review of taxation and finances on behalf of the Joint Select Committee, in which he concluded that Africans, while carrying more than their share of the burden, were receiving much less than their due of expenditures (5). In recommending an income tax for Europeans and a special fund for African development, the Moyne Commission issued a direct challenge to the common assumption that the primacy of Europeans could be justified by the high proportion of their contribution to the development of the territory. Thus, British policy, as developed in concrete actions as well as in policy statements, increasingly emphasized its ultimate responsibility for the destiny of the African people of Kenya. But while the settlers' cause may by this time already have been defeated, they still had many battles to win, and continued in various ways to increase their influence in the Government of the colony. African paramountcy was to remain purely theoretical until well into the 1950's, and many Europeans continued to indulge their extravagant hopes right up to the eve of Independence.

EDUCATION: COOPERATION BETWEEN
GOVERNMENT AND MISSIONS

Against this background of political agitation, education during the interwar years was shaped by increasing Government involvement, primarily through its support of missionary schools. As is the case in defining any historical period, the choice of a date marking the start of this involvement is somewhat arbitrary. The appointment of J. Nelson Frazer in 1909 as advisor on education to the governments of British East Africa may be considered to signal the end of the mission's virtual monopoly in the field of education (6). Frazer, who had been the principal of a training college in Bombay, urged the Government to take a greater responsibility for the education of all races in Kenya by establishing a Department of Education. Frazer looked upon the African population as an important source of manpower for the European community and recommended "industrial education" as the most appropriate form of training for Africans (7).

When the Department of Education was established with James R. Orr as its first Director, it marked the Government's first significant educational commitment. Because the First World War soon absorbed most of the territory's energies and resources, it was not until 1918 that education again received governmental attention. In that year, at Orr's urging, the Governor appointed an Education Commission "to consider [the] . . . backward state of education of all races in this Protectorate (8)." An indication of this backwardness was the estimate given in a 1919 Census that 30,000 Africans out of a 2.7 million population were attending 410 mission schools (9). The entire budget of the Education Department was £636.

The 1919 Commission sought testimony from a broad segment of the European population, whose evidence provides a wealth of data on European attitudes towards Africans, as well as recording opinions of what the schools could and should do. The general feeling was one of relief that the Government had finally stepped in to assume responsibility for education. Many witnesses said the Department's primary concern should be the education of European children, and frequent reference was made to the

---

EDUCATION DEPARTMENT BUDGET 1919 (10)

Director (European)	£500
Head Clerk (African)	32
Assistant Clerk (Indian)	72
Assistant Clerk (African)	32
Total	636

"bad influence" of the natives and to the effects of living in the tropics putting a "strain on the brain (11)."

H. R. Montgomery, the District Commissioner of Kitui, spoke for many administrators in urging more concern with the development of the reserves, in the patronizing language that now seems so distasteful: ". . . for some years to come he [the African] must be regarded as a child and, as such, not allowed to decide what is best for himself. . . . It is our duty to educate the native whatever his inclinations may be (12)."

Most of the witnesses expressed various forms of self-interest in recognizing that the education of the African community could benefit all residents of the territory. The economists' view of education as an investment that can yield important returns to the state has only been accepted widely since 1960 (13), and it is remarkable that Orr's testimony before the Commission several decades earlier often reflected this approach. After producing comparative data from other territories on the proportion of Government expenditures devoted to education, showing the East Africa Protectorate at the bottom, Orr made a chauvinistic appeal for more educational effort:

I would therefore impress upon all who have the control of education: (1) that the most thoughtfully educated nation will in the future rule the world, (2) that the physical, moral, intellectual and vocational training of every boy and girl throughout the Protectorate increases the manpower and resources of the Empire (14).

What this meant in practice was academic education for Europeans and, for Africans, industrial training after an academic primary education, based on the model established for American Negroes by Booker T. Washington, among others (15).

While the 1919 Commission urged the Government to play a larger role in education, the underlying assumption, often stated explicitly, was that the missions would continue to run most of the schools. Basing their argument for the continued dominance of the missions on the importance of building character through religious training, the council recommended that all mission schools be registered and subsidized by grade; that teachers be graded by qualifying examinations, and their salaries subsidized; and that the Government provide scholarships for students (16). Despite the strong objections of a priest in Kisumi, who argued that religion was the primary purpose of mission schools and that Government assistance would imply control (17), the Representative Council of the Allied Missionary Societies urged direct Government aid.

In 1922 the Education Department officially established a grant-in-aid system by which mission schools judged to meet certain standards received financial aid (18). The development of the grant-in-aid pattern received international support from the Commissions of the Phelps-Stokes Fund in

1919 and 1924, which focused attention on the dismal state of education for Africans from both the quantitative and qualitative viewpoints. The Phelps-Stokes Report on East Africa emphasized the need for greater cooperation between governments and missions, and urged that academic systems be adapted to African needs (19). While these ideas remained poorly defined for many years, there has been general agreement among those concerned with African education that the Phelps-Stokes Reports made a major contribution to the formation of colonial policy, not by developing new ideas but by drawing together the growing awareness of the problems into a comprehensive and constructive critique (20). However, some observers were critical that the Reports' emphasis on adaptation of European education to African needs assumed a static peasant society in a permanently inferior position (21).

In 1925 the Colonial Office established a permanent Advisory Committee on Education, whose first report to the Secretary of State drew heavily upon the Phelps-Stokes Reports (22). The official policy statement of the Advisory Committee, the 1925 Memorandum, established 13 broad principles which, according to most observers, "have become the basic structure upon which subsequent educational proposals have been built (23)." In response to the criticism that African education was too much removed from the traditions and the realities of tribal life, the Memorandum stated:

Education should be adapted to the mentality, aptitudes, occupations, and traditions of the various peoples, conserving so far as possible all sound and healthy elements in the fabric of their social life; adapting them where necessary to changed circumstances and progressive ideas, as an agent of natural growth and evolution. Its aim should be to render the individual more efficient in his or her condition of life, whatever it may be, and to promote the advancement of the community as a whole through the improvement of agriculture, the development of native industries, the improvement of health, the training of people in the management of their own affairs, and the circulation of true ideals of citizenship and service (24).

Because so many of the principles of the 1925 Memorandum have been reiterated since it was first formulated, a brief review of some of the major points will be useful. In order to assure sufficient numbers of qualified teachers, inspectors, and supervisors, the report stressed that efforts should be made to recruit staff from overseas, in addition to accelerating training of African staff. In keeping with the general aim of fitting education to the local needs, it stated that African vernaculars should be preserved, and textbooks and methodology adapted to the African situation. Following the example of the Jeanes school founded at Kabete, Kenya, earlier in the year (25), the 1925 Memorandum encouraged the development of specially-trained visiting teachers for village schools. Acknowledging that the education of women and girls had lagged seriously behind that of men, it called for increased efforts in this area on the grounds that educated wives and mothers would contribute to the general welfare of the home and community. Looking at the educational system as a whole, the Memorandum (26) cited the importance of developing an entire range of facilities, from infant education to institutions which might eventually attain university status, including specialized training in medicine and agriculture as well as in general areas which came to be called community development (27). To achieve these aims, the Memorandum called for the establishment of educational advisory boards in each territory, representing the various voluntary agencies (and in Kenya, the settlers as well), but under the responsibility of the Government. The element of cooperation was to be maintained by the grant-in-aid system of subsidizing the approved mission schools. In addition to the utilitarian advantage of using the personnel and facilities already available, working through the missions reflected the continuing emphasis upon religion and character training (28).

The policy of adapting European education to the African setting was far more significant—and far more controversial—than the pragmatic decision to subsidize mission schools had been. In analyzing the goal of adapting education to the local needs, Margaret Read remarked:

It is impossible to escape from the conclusion that the authors of the 1925 Memorandum believed . . . that some kind of sifting process could take place, and . . . all that was "best" would come through the sieve and be used in the schools, and that what was "defective" and did not get through, could be conveniently and quietly thrown away (29).

While Professor Read's comments constitute a harsh criticism of a genuine effort to make an irrelevant system more relevant to the needs of rural societies, they suggest fundamental weaknesses in the assumptions underlying the 1925 Memorandum. Traditional society no longer existed as a relatively stable entity which could be preserved; the complex of forces accompanying colonial rule was rapidly breaking down the very institutions that the Memorandum sought to build upon. At the same time the vocational bias of African education, regardless of its motivation, was understandably seen by the African as a second-rate, inferior education designed to keep him in his place. This was particularly true in Kenya, with its legislative prohibition against the independent participation of Africans in many kinds of cash-crop farming. Widespread opposition developed among Africans to the missionary-educators' introduction of school gardens, with an emphasis on "traditional" agriculture, which further emphasized the political and racial basis of the educational system (30).

The dilemma of determining what was a relevant education for Africans paralleled the debate between W.E.B. DuBois and Booker T. Washington regarding the appropriate form of education for the American Negro (31). In both Africa and the United States, official policy makers favored a vocational emphasis, but because vocational training was usually considered an inferior education by parents and students, practice rarely followed policy. There can be little doubt that prior to Independence, colonial efforts to develop rural vocational education were generally unsuccessful, primarily because education cannot be isolated in a vacuum, but must instead be seen in the context of society at large. Given the racial stratification of the colonial system and the far greater opportunities for wage-employment out of the reserves than in them, it is hardly surprising that "special" education for Africans was regarded as inferior to academic education (32).

With the development of the grant-in-aid system, a symbiotic relationship emerged between the mission schools and the Government. In 1926, the Education Department acknowledged that because of "the inability of the Government to meet and satisfy a mass movement throughout the Colony in favour of education . . . the missions stepped into the breach (33)." By 1949 the shoe was on the other foot and the Education Department recalled that the "Grant-in Aid Rules were made necessary by the fact that the missions were faced with educational commitments beyond their ability to support (34)." Regardless of the initial basis for the relationship between the Government and the voluntary agencies, their cooperation had become increasingly formalized since 1911. The missions assumed major responsibility for primary and secondary education, the Government for higher education and technical subjects (35), a division which was confirmed at the Le Zoute Conference of Protestant Missions in 1926 (36).

Cooperation among the various missionary bodies proved more difficult to achieve than between the missionaries and Government. The first important breakthrough in this area was the establishment of the Alliance High School in 1926, by an alliance of Protestant missions. Further progress was made in 1928 and 1929 at an interterritorial education conference held in Dar Es Salaam, Tanganyika, to adopt a uniform organization for schools and a common language policy (37).

This period of cooperation gradually brought about a number of changes in mission education. The "out stations," or "bush schools," which were usually of a very informal nature, became primary schools. Schools for catechists became teacher training centers, and boarding schools at the mission stations frequently became secondary schools. These changes were accompanied by certain sacrifices on the part of some of the missions; Africans tended to prefer the financial returns of teaching to a career in the ministry, and many missionaries who had formerly devoted only part of their time to educational activities found themselves working full time at what had originally been a supplementary concern (38). Although motivation varied considerably, many missionaries viewed their educational role as a means of evangelization, rather than as an end in itself. At the same time, Africans came to see education as the key to economic and social progress, with missionary cooperation as the means of achieving education. Thus, another

73001

symbiotic relationship developed between the missions and the Africans, in which education was the key ingredient.

Racial Stratification

The racial caste system which was taking shape in Kenya was reflected in subsequent educational developments. Despite the British Government's recognition of the paramountcy of African interests, the colony's political development did not undergo immediate changes, and European settlers steadily entrenched their superior position during the years between the wars. The establishment in 1924 of separate education advisory committees for the three racial groups in the colony formalized the means by which the immigrant communities shaped their educational systems, and the educational patterns reflected the relative strengths of these vested interests (39). Not only was the expenditure per pupil more than five times higher for Europeans than for Africans, but when seen in relation to the total population, the imbalances were even greater (40).

Still more important than the quantitative imbalances were the qualitative factors which shaped African education during the period. The 1926 Annual Report of the Education Department reveals the inherent inconsistencies in official policy by calling on Europeans to set a good example for Africans, stating that "if we of the superior race" behave badly, the Africans cannot be blamed for following suit; the same report also states that "much of the difficulty of the period in African education arises from . . . the inferiority complex in the native mind (41)."

1926 EDUCATION DEPARTMENT EXPENDITURE BY RACE[a]

Race	Pupils[b]	Expenditure[c] (in U.S. dollars)	Expenditure per pupil
African[d]	6,948	232,293	33.4
Asian	1,900	70,329	37
European	776	140,041	180.5
Total	9,624	442,663	46

[a]Excluding "administrative" and "extraordinary" expenditure.
[b]State and state-aided schools only.
[c]Based on exchange rate of $4.86 per pound.
[d]Including Arabs.

Source: Kenya, Education Department, *Annual Report, 1930* (Nairobi: Government Printer, 1931), pp. 9-10.

In order to adapt education to the "mentality, aptitudes, occupations and traditions" of Africans, as the 1925 Memorandum directed, the 1926 Annual Report identified "Three clearly marked sections of the community (1) the great mass of village life in the native Reserves, (2) the artisans and craftsmen of the community generally, and (3) the educated and skilled professions required by the State and commerce (42)." The Report went on to describe the goals of education in terms of what would today be considered manpower planning: ". . . the aim of African education in Kenya is, firstly to study the composition and the needs of the community as a whole and then to direct the pupils that they may find a sphere of usefulness in one section or another, and to prevent as far as possible the wastage of human effort by the creation of misfits (43)."

The statement would be a suitable goal for any educational system were it not for its underlying assumptions concerning the African's intellectual potential: "Just as handwork has been found useful in the training of mentally defective children, so the most useful training which the African can receive in his present condition is continued contact with material processes (44)." Aside from carrying the Phelps-Stokes reaction against literary education to the extreme, such a statement reveals the racist attitudes which shaped Government policy during the 1920's.

The Report went on to describe the type of education that would be suitable for the first of the three levels, citing the role of the Jeanes schools:

for the improvement of village life . . . where Africans of high character and tactful disposition, but not of high intellectual attainments are being trained as supervisors of village schools. The object of their training is to keep the education of the rural school closely in touch with rural requirements and to avoid giving village children an education which will divorce them from interest in village life and cause them to seek employment in the towns (45).

The Jeanes movement took its name from a philanthropic Quaker lady of Philadelphia, Pennsylvania, who had supported Negro education in the American South in the early 1900's. The first Jeanes school in Africa was started at Kabete, Kenya in 1925 as a direct result of the Phelps-Stokes Commission Report, with financial assistance from the Carnegie Corporation of New York. The essence of the Jeanes movement was the realization that formal education could reach only a small segment of African society and that grass-roots efforts at the village level were required to reach the mass of population. Jeanes teachers served the total community, with husbands and wives posted as a team. The village women were instructed in health and sanitation, child care, and general home economics, while the men's teachers emphasized practical demonstration of agricultural techniques. This concentration on the .informal education of adults and community development gained momentum during the 1930's, and Jeanes schools were established throughout Africa (46). Despite being criticized both for doing too little and for trying to do too much (47), the Jeanes movement attracted many enthusiastic admirers (48).

The technical school at Machakos and the Native Industrial Training Depot established at Kabete in 1925 were intended to establish a pattern for the creation of an artisan class for the territory as a whole. Progress in the field of technical training was hampered, it was said, by "the present stage of the mental development of the African (49)." The Government's condescending attitude is revealed in the following remark: "We wish to lead him [the African] to citizenship by a more efficient route than seditious rebellion. . . . Even if a student chooses a sedentary occupation it will not harm him to be able to repair the chair he sits in (50)."

At the top level of the system, in the skilled professions, it is interesting to note that the economic position of the African was less clearly defined than his social or political status. "The demand of the State and of commerce for a more highly educated class of individuals who can take their place as leaders among the Africans or within the ranks of the community as thinkers and professional workers is met at the Alliance High School, Kikuyu (51)."

Although the first two years of study at Alliance High School consisted of a "literary" curriculum, including English, arithmetic, and general science, the emphasis after the third year was distinctly vocational, in keeping with the general European belief in the African's limited intellectual capacity (52). Educational practice thus lagged behind official colonial policy of protecting the paramountcy of African interests within a predominantly settler economy.

The three-tiered pattern which emerged in Kenya, with community development for the majority, technical training for a minority, and academic secondary education for a tiny fraction of the African population, was reinforced by subsequent policy statements of the British Colonial Office. In 1935, the Advisory Committee issued its second major policy statement regarding African education, *The Education of African Communities* (53). The 1935 Memorandum, as it came to be called, closely followed its 1925 counterpart, but stressed the interrelationship of the schools with other aspects of community life, such as adult education, health, and agriculture (54). In 1943, the Advisory Committee issued its third major policy memorandum, *Mass Education in African Society*, which stated broader concern for the welfare of the entire community (55). Pointing to universal schooling for children as a long-range goal, the 1943 Memorandum also stressed the importance of adult literacy and coordinated welfare plans for the benefit of the entire community. The idea of mass education, essentially a continuation and expansion of the themes expressed in the 1925 Memorandum, was later adopted by UNESCO under the term "fundamental education (56)."

0354624

The policy statements consistently recommended community development for the bulk of the African population. After Independence, the efforts of several African countries, Tanzania in particular, to reorient their inherited educational systems towards rural needs often echo these earlier policies. Under the Colonial Government, however, such efforts were typically regarded as offering inferior education. What is perhaps most. significant about the frequently cited memoranda of 1925, 1935, and 1943 is not simply that they were unpopular, but that in ignoring the felt needs of the Africans, the policy statements had remarkably little effect on actual developments.

THE AFRICAN RESPONSE TO COLONIAL RULE

In the assertion that Speke "discovered" the source of the Nile and in the arguments over who should serve as trustee for the Africans, the assumption—implicit or explicit—was that the African himself need not be considered (57). Even after the declaration by the Government of the paramountcy of African interests in 1923, colonial policy was characterized by negative paternalism rather than commitment to the development of the African community.

In the area of "Native Administration," the Colonial Government never succeeded in establishing the credibility of the chiefs it appointed. Throughout British-ruled Africa, the theory of indirect rule, first developed by Sir Frederick Lugard in Northern Nigeria in the early 1900's (58), was often cited as the cornerstone of administrative policy. Sir Donald Cameron introduced the concept in Tanganyika during the 1920's, and in that territory the British governed the African population through existing tribal institutions. The policy, which was a pragmatic means of getting by with a minimum number of European administrators, also stressed the preservation of essential aspects of the local culture. Cameron states the principle as:

adopting for the purposes of local government the institutions which the native people have evolved for themselves, so that they may develop in a constitutional manner from their own past, guided and restrained by the traditions and sanctions which they have inherited, moulded or modified as they may be on the advice of British officers (59).

Cameron was enough of a realist to warn against setting up a figurehead or puppet authority where no such figure had existed formerly, stressing that indirect rule was a means of developing the African population and not an end in itself (60). But in Kenya, where there were very few ethnic groups who had paramount chiefs, attempts to implant indirect rule often made traditional society still less "democratic" than in neighboring colonies. British-appointed chiefs had "no traditional sanction and to a large extent they were regarded merely as the lackeys of a foreign conqueror (61)." The failure of the British to recognize the political consequences of establishing collaborators is exemplified in a statement by a District Commissioner of Machakos that "chiefs who stand by the government get left by their people who are unable to see ahead like their chiefs (62)."

Because of its "belief in indefinite time ahead (63)," the Colonial Government made no effort to build an African political framework on a national scale, and attempts to implant indirect rule not only fostered tribalism but forced African protest movements to operate outside the legal framework.

Until the mid-1960's, most historical studies of the period between the world wars concentrated on the official views expressed in policy statements. However, revisionist interpretations have been put forward by Terence Ranger and others, who draw attention to the long-overlooked role of the Africans in influencing events (64). It is beyond the scope of this study to examine the many facets of African politics except as they directly effect educational development (65). However, the growing initiative of those Africans most affected by the European presence during the 1920's and 1930's had a profound influence on such development.

The relation of these initiatives to educational development must be seen within the context of administrative changes (66). In 1924, an amendment to the Native Authority Ordinance authorized the central Government to establish Local Native Councils in the reserves. These Councils were generally considered a step in the right direction by the Africans, because representatives of their own choosing, subject to the approval of the District Officer, could raise and administer funds for local projects such as road construction and education (67). However, attempts to integrate these councils with the existing traditional authorities were frequently unsuccessful, as many Africans under the Councils' jurisdiction referred their grievances to the recognized elders rather than to the authorities established by the central Government.

The Ordinance of 1931, which established School Area Committees on which Local Native Council members were to be represented, might have greatly stimulated African participation in education, but due to the lack of supervisory staff, the plan was not put into practice. A similar problem resulted in 1934, when the newly created District Education Boards, which included representatives of the Government, missions, and Local Native Councils, were unable to carry out their supervisory functions because of insufficient financial support (68). Thus, the pattern of trusteeship that emerged in the mid-1930's was one of word rather than deed. Despite the alleged British desire to preserve the best of the traditional culture, there was a growing realization on the part of most observers that little was actually being done to prepare Africans to assume a paramount place within Kenyan society.

African Initiatives

It is not surprising that the first African political tactics developed among the tribes most closely affected by Europeans: the Kikuyu near the central highlands and, to a lesser extent, the Luo of Nyanza Province near Lake Victoria. Contact with the Europeans generated many specific grievances and also provided an opportunity to learn the Europeans' ways, both through formal schooling and by observing the settlers' political techniques. The possibility of direct political action within the Legislative Council was denied to the Africans, yet their early attempts to influence the Colonial Government through other channels were modeled on the settlers' Convention of Associations.

The first such organization was the Kikuyu Association, formed largely at Government urging in 1920 by the trusted Government-appointed chiefs as a buffer between tribal grievances and the central Government. It was followed in 1921 by a very different type of pressure group, the Young Kikuyu Association (YKA), whose leader, Harry Thuku, went over the heads of the chiefs and presented grievances, mainly on wage questions, directly to the Governments in Nairobi and London (69). Thuku tried to establish a broad, intertribal coalition of interests—primarily over issues of land, labor, and taxation—but he was arrested and detained in 1922 for his role as an agitator. Thuku's arrest touched off a massive demonstration of some 7,000 or 8,000 persons at the Nairobi Police Station to demand his release. Accounts vary as to the exact causes and course of the ensuing events, but apparently the crowd provoked police retaliation, and more than 20 Africans were killed (70).

Despite efforts by Archdeacon Owen of the Church Missionary Society and others to direct future protest movements into officially acceptable channels, splits inevitably developed between moderate and militant factions, and the initiative gradually shifted to the more militant groups (71). In 1925 a shift in the leadership of the Kikuyu tribe brought younger men to the helm of the Kikuyu Central Association (KCA), which grew out of the Young Kikuyu Association. The KCA petitioned the Government on a variety of subjects, including the release of Thuku, and the right of Africans to grow coffee (72). Thuku was elected president of the KCA after his release from prison in 1930, but his influence was somewhat diminished as younger leaders emerged. Johnstone (later Jomo) Kenyatta was very active in the KCA, and was sent by the Association to England to present African demands concerning taxation (73).

Without examining the evolution of Kenya's political forces in detail, certain generalizations can be made which place into perspective many of the factors which later shaped educational developments (74). First, the Government was in no hurry to encourage African participation on the national political scene. The political outlets fostered by the Local Native Councils and indirect rule were often bypassed because they did not meet the requirements of traditional society. Thus, most political development "was forced into channels of permanent opposition to established authority, whether the authority was the European government or the elders who appeared to the younger men to be the tools of the European government (75)."

Secondly, despite the growing splits within the African political movement, better educational facilities became a universal demand of all the factions. The Kikuyu concentrated their efforts in this direction on the establishment of the Kikuyu Independent Schools' Association (KISA) in 1929. In part, the KISA represented a reaction against the policy of the Church of Scotland and several other missions prohibiting the traditional practice of female circumcision (76), one instance of direct conflict between European and traditional culture. Significantly, the Africans, by establishing the KISA, were in a sense following the principles of the 1925 Memorandum by adapting the schools and churches to their own culture. Since African education was primarily carried out by the missions, the so-called independent church movement and independent school movement were closely interrelated, and I shall use the terms synonymously.

CULTURAL NATIONALISM: THE INDEPENDENT SCHOOLS

Although some small factions within the independent school movement were extremely anti-Western, the general emphasis was not anti-Christian. However, Africans increasingly asked themselves whether it was necessary to give up important aspects of their traditional culture in order to be Christian (77). The goal of the separatist movement was thus selection of some elements of European culture for adaptation to the African culture. Welbourn identifies four ways in which the independent churches accomplished this task: they retained female circumcision and polygamy; baptism and other aspects of Christianity were adapted to suit African conditions; education was vital, but Africanization was too, and there was less emphasis on British history and literature; and both religion and schooling stressed the importance of land (78).

The movement had begun in the so-called out-schools of Kiambu district, as the Africans boycotted missionaries who opposed female circumcision (79). Soon, however, the KISA and its offshoots had developed an entire school system independent of the missions. Every effort was made to build education upon the new African attitudes of independent thought; for this purpose a teacher training college was established at Githunguri, which rejected the Government syllabus and examinations, and substituted its own (80).

Much has been made of the connection between the independent school movement and the Mau Mau rebellion of the 1950's. Mau Mau and the origins of nationalism in Kenya are discussed later in this book, but it is useful at this point to indicate some of the social and political forces that underlay the religious and educational changes of the period. Welbourn notes that since there were few legally recognized means by which progressive young Kikuyu could present their grievances, the "thwarted political drive was to find its own institutional expression in the independent churches (81)." Rosberg and Nottingham consider what they call cultural nationalism (82) to have been a replacement for discussion of such concrete issues as land and labor policies, and thus a substitute avenue of political expression; Jomo Kenyatta's *Facing Mount Kenya* exemplifies this (83). According to Welbourn, the issue of female circumcision "was no more than an emotional peg onto which a far wider area of social discontent could readily be hung. It enabled a general unrest and desire for independence to be focused at a point—in the churches and church schools—where rules could be disobeyed and independence asserted with the least danger of interference by an all-powerful government (84)."

The response of the Government to cultural nationalism was ambivalent. At first the Government looked upon the boycotting of mission schools as a vote of confidence for nondenominational Government schools (85) rather than as an African separatist movement. But by 1931, it acknowledged the problem of controlling and supervising the rapidly growing movement (86), and the New Education Ordinance of that year gave much greater representation to Africans on the Local Native Councils. Soon the Government was making "every effort to cooperate with the independent schools while attempting to exercise some form of control by financial grants-in-aid through Local Native Councils (87)." Although the Government was only dimly aware of what L. J. Lewis called the "revolutionary" nature of the social and political forces behind the independent schools movement (88), the creation of District Education Boards in 1934 was further acknowledgement by the Government of the need to allow greater participation by Africans in the running of primary schools, while preserving some degree of central control. The District Education Boards, consisting of Africans nominated by the Local Councils, representatives of district school managers (usually missionaries), and Government officials, were empowered to allocate funds from local and central Government sources to primary schools, subject to approval by the Director of Education (89).

Financial constraints resulting from the world depression during the 1930's made supervision and control of the independent schools difficult. By 1936, the Government estimated that five percent of the total African student population was in the independent schools, with the overwhelming majority of these in Kikuyu areas (90). In the same year, the Government took steps to achieve a rapprochement with the independent schools. A meeting between representatives of the independent schools and the missions

produced an agreement that would have brought the former into the official
orbit of Government-maintained and assisted schools by tighter supervision
and inspection (91). Although the agreement specified that no new schools
would be opened until the existing ones had been approved by the Education
Department, the rapid expansion of independent schools in 1937 and 1938
indicated that the attempt at rapprochement had failed (92). However, in
1937, after the KISA had agreed to use the Government syllabus, an
Inspector of Schools with special responsibility for the independent schools
was appointed.

Changing Attitudes

In retrospect, one of the most significant aspects of the independent
school movement was that it forced the Government and the missions to
reconsider some of the basic assumptions underlying their policies. The
African community would no longer tolerate mere paternalism, and now
demanded an increasing share in the running of their schools. However, the
depression and the threat of war curtailed major advances in African
education during the 1930's. Mission education came under increasing
criticism, not only from African separatist movements but from European
educators who questioned the system's efficiency. It had become evident that
insufficient funds were available for supervision, so that aid was granted
without developing a uniform standard of education. In 1938 Wallbank
wrote:

The Missionary Societies have been the educational pioneers in Kenya
and have rendered a distinguished service. But there are certain weaknesses
inherent in a system which utilizes seventeen distinct, and at times hostile,
bodies in carrying on what is primarily a responsibility of the state (93).

Despite such occasional rumblings, the fact remained that because the
Government lacked personnel and funds, there was no alternative to
continuing the policy of cooperation with the missions. This was confirmed
in 1940 by the report of a committee appointed by the Kenya Missionary
Council to review educational policy. The report reiterated themes which had
been identified since before World War I: namely, the need for greater
cooperation between the Government and the missions, and the particular
importance of developing the entire community and expanding the education
of girls (94). As in the past, however, such statements of policy had minimal
impact on education practice.

HIGHER EDUCATION AND POLICY CHANGES

After the 1935 Memorandum, the next milestone of educational policy
came in the previously neglected area of higher education. Largely through

the efforts of Sir Philip Mitchell, the Governor of Uganda, the Colonial Office appointed a commission in 1937 (95) to look into the needs and possibilities for higher education in Africa. Although the report was criticized for being too narrowly vocational in its stress on technical education (96), it recommended that Makerere College, established in 1922 as a school for skilled trades, be developed as rapidly as possible into a university (97).

After conducting a survey of vocational-technical education in 1940 (98), the Colonial Office appointed a Commission in 1943, under the chairmanship of Asquith, to reexamine the needs of higher education in the colonies. In striking contrast to the 1937 de la Warr Commission, the Asquith Commission played down the vocational role of higher education and stressed the importance of the university in providing men trained for public service and professional careers (99). The report went on to recommend the creation of an Inter-University Council for Higher Education in the Colonies to develop colonial institutions closely affiliated with the University of London. Thus, the most significant impact of the Asquith Commission upon educational policy was in shifting emphasis from the vocational to the academic (100).

A CRITICAL SUMMARY

The Colonial Development and Welfare Act of 1945 marked a significant shift from the traditional policy of colonial economic self-sufficiency to a policy of giving increased amounts of aid to the colonies. The war years marked not only a shift in economic policy but also revealed a desire on the part of the British Government to create a more progressive political situation in the colonies. In an effort to get away from the somewhat negative, paternalistic connotations of "trusteeship," the Colonial Office introduced the term "partnership," to indicate a less static relationship between the races (101), and partnership became a controversial issue in later attempts to build multiracial governments in East and Central Africa. The most significant contribution to educational policy during the partnership era was the 1948 Memorandum, *Education for Citizenship*. This document went beyond previous statements by stating that literacy and technical skills were not enough in a rapidly changing world. It stated that education must develop a sense of "public responsibility (102)," and democracy must be lived, not just taught in a classroom. By this assertion, *Education for Citizenship* gave a political dimension to educational policy which, although totally inadequate for the situation, indicated an awareness of the African's growing political role.

Despite apparently progressive policy statements, education in Kenya suffered badly during World War II, and the gap between goals and realities remained wide. Besides diverting funds from social services, the war took much-needed supervisory staff from the Government and the missions, and many African teachers were attracted by higher wages in other occupations. Combined with the growing forces of change within the African community, this resulted in rapid expansion of the Government-aided school system, with a corresponding decline in quality because of the lack of control or supervision (103).

The grant-in-aid rules of 1945 attempted to control expansion by stopping additions to the list of aided schools, but expenditures continued to rise as the previously-aided schools doubled in size and added staff (104). The new regulations also placed the financial responsibility for primary schools upon the Local Native Councils and tried to set standards by making the salaries of teachers in aided schools equal to those in Government schools. Nevertheless, the expansion continued almost unchecked (105).

An analysis of the 1949 Annual Report of the Education Department reveals a number of problems. Although roughly 25 percent of the primary school-aged population were enrolled in schools, more than one-third of these pupils were in unaided institutions without regulated standards, and approximately 60 percent of all the students completed only two years of school (106). The system's high wastage, or dropout rate, continued so that only five percent received more than six years of schooling and less than one percent went beyond the eighth year. The imbalances were even more exaggerated because of the small percentage of girls, which fell from 30 percent of total enrollment in the first year to less than seven percent at the end of the fourteenth (107).

In addition to the uncontrolled expansion, extreme wastage within the educational pyramid, and disparities between the geographical regions and between the sexes, there were continued inequalities in the separate facilities provided for the territory's racial communities. The 1923 statement of African paramountcy had had relatively little effect upon the settlers' domination of the economy. In 1948, when there were approximately 300 times as many school-age Africans in Kenya as there were school-age Europeans, the central Government's expenditures for the two groups were almost identical (108).

However, the contribution to African education made by the Local Native Councils rose from £77,753 in 1946 to £158,656 in 1949 (109). Furthermore, as a result of the 1945 Colonial Development and Welfare Act, and Kenya's Ten-Year Development Program which followed in 1948 (110), Education Department expenditures on African education exceeded expenditures on European education in 1948 for the first time. The Ten-Year Plan called for providing 50 percent of the school-age population with a six-year primary course at the end of a ten-year period. In order to achieve this expansion, local expenditure would have to increase from £100,000 to £343,000, while the central Government would contribute £800,000 for capital costs, mostly buildings (111). In the same year that the Ten-Year Plan was published, the Report of the Salaries Commission went into effect, entailing "large increases in the salaries of Government African teachers (112)." Since the Local Native Councils found it impossible to finance both the salary increases and the proposed expansion, the result was that quantity once more won out over quality, and expansion at the primary level continued almost unchecked. The 1949 Annual Report of the Education Department noted that by that year "the Local Native Councils found themselves more than half-way to the financial target set for them in 1957 by the Ten-Year Plan (113)." Faced with this evidence of uncontrolled expansion, the Governor appointed a committee in January, 1949, under the chairmanship of the Venerable Archdeacon L. J. Beecher of Mombasa, to examine and report on "the scope, content and methods of the African educational system (114)." In addition to Archdeacon Beecher, the Committee included several churchmen—indicating to some extent the continuing importance of the missions in shaping educational policies—and only one African, the Honorable Eliud Mathu (115). The Committee's findings, published in September, 1949, served as the framework for educational planning in Kenya during the 1950's.

Notes

1. The traditional colonial histories generally saw the movement towards independence as a paternalistic development of the natives until they were eventually "ready," while recent revisionist interpretations of Kenya's colonial history place greater emphasis on the response of the African community. See particularly Ogot and Kieran (eds.), *Zamani: A Survey of East African History* (Nairobi: East African Publishing House, 1968); Carl Rosberg, Jr. and John Nottingham, *The Myth of Mau Mau: Nationalism in Kenya* (New York: Praeger, 1966).

2. Great Britain Colonial Office, *Indians in Kenya,* Cmd. 1922 (London: H.M.S.O., 1923), p. 9.

3. Great Britain Colonial Office, *Report of the Commission on Closer Union of the Dependencies in Eastern and Central Africa,* Cmd. 3234 (London: H.M.S.O., 1929). During the 1930's and 1940's there were several more attempts to achieve closer union. The only real progress was in the area of economic cooperation (common postal services, customs union, etc.), culminating in 1948 with the creation of the High Commission (now the East African Community). Political unification has so far made little headway. For more detail see Donald S. Rothchild, *Toward Unity in Africa* (Washington: Public Affairs Press, 1960), pp. 15-86; Carl G. Rosberg, Jr. with Aaron Segal, "An East African Federation", *International Conciliation,* no. 543 (New York: Carnegie Endowment for International Peace, May 1963), pp. 12-16; A. J. Hughes, *East Africa: The Search for Unity* (Baltimore: Penguin Books, 1963). The best treatment to date is Donald S. Rothchild, *The Politics of Integration* (Nairobi: East African Publishing House, 1968).

4. G. Bennett, *Kenya: A Political History*, p. 76.

5. Great Britain Colonial Office, *Report of the Financial Commissioner on Certain Questions in Kenya*, Cmd. 4093 (London: H.M.S.O., 1932), p. 38 (Moyne Commission).

6. East African Protectorate, *Education Report, 1909* (Nairobi: Government Printer, 1909), p. 1.

7. *Ibid.*, p. 33.

8. East African Protectorate, *Report of the Education Commission of the East African Protectorate* (Nairobi: The Surft Press, 1919), p. 169; hereafter referred to as the 1919 Commission.

9. East African Standard, *The "Standard" British East Africa and Uganda Handbook and Directory* (Nairobi: East African Standard, 1919), pp. 163, 164.

10. 1919 Commission, *op. cit.*, p. 189.

11. *Ibid.*, pp. 49, 138.

12. *Ibid.*, p. 128.

13. See Chapter VI for a description of the investment approach in educational planning.

14. 1919 Commission, *op. cit.*, p. 171.

15. *Ibid.*, p. 185.

16. *Ibid.*, p. 97.

17. *Ibid.*, pp. 22, 23.

18. Kenya Colony and Protectorate, *Departmental Instructions Concerning Native Education in Assisted Schools* (Nairobi: Government Printer, 1922).

19. Thomas Jesse Jones, *Education in East Africa* (London: Edinburgh House Press, 1925, also published in New York by the Phelps-Stokes Fund), p. 118.

20. See L. J. Lewis (ed.), *The Phelps-Stokes Reports on Education in Africa*, abr. (London: Oxford University Press, 1962).

21. A. Victor Murray, *The School in the Bush* (London: Longmans, 1929), pp. 291-311. See also Norman Leys, *Kenya* (London: The Hogarth Press, 1924), pp. 390-392.

22. L. J. Lewis, *Educational Policy and Practice in British Tropical Areas* (London: Nelson and Sons, Ltd., 1954), p. 13.

23. David G. Scanlon, "Education and Nationalism in Kenya and the Gold Coast," *Teachers College Record*, LVI, no. 6 (March, 1955), 339.

24. Great Britain Colonial Office, *Educational Policy in British Tropical Africa*, Cmd. 2347 (London: H.M.S.O., 1925), p. 4.

25. The Jeanes School Movement is discussed later in this chapter.

26. The 1925 Memorandum was only eight pages. For a summary of the 13 principles, see Cambridge Conference, p. 3.

27. It is beyond the scope of this study to examine the implications of the changing terminology which referred to the recognition that schools for youth were not enough. Fundamental education, basic education, community education, adult education, and other terms all gained acceptance at various times as means of developing the knowledge, skills, and attitudes of communities at large.

28. Although to Americans the relationship between religion and education is a sensitive subject, it is useful to recall that in Britain, as in many other countries, there was a long tradition of government support of church schools, and religious and character training were considered vital parts of a sound education.

29. Margaret Read, *Education and Cultural Traditions* (London: University of London, Institute of Education, 1950), Studies in Education, no. 2, p. 9.

30. Kenneth J. King, *The Politics of Agricultural Education for Africans in Kenya,* paper presented at Historical Association of Kenya, Annual Conference, 1969, mimeo.

31. For an analysis of these contrasting views, seen in relation to African education, see Edward Berman, *Education in Africa and America: A History of the Phelps-Stokes Fund, 1911-1945* (New York: Teachers College, Columbia University, unpublished, 1969). Also King, "Africa and the Southern States of the U.S.A.: Notes on J. H. Oldham and American Negro Education for Africans," *Journal of African History,* X, no. 4, (1969), 659-677.

32. James J. Shields, Jr., *The Reports of the Phelps-Stokes Fund on Education in Africa and the Formation of a Theory of Community Development by the British* (New York: Phelps-Stokes Fund, Occasional Paper no. 4, May 4, 1961), pp. 6, 7; also W. A. Dodd, *"Education for Self-Reliance" in Tanzania* (New York: Teachers College Press, 1969).

33. Kenya Colony and Protectorate, *Education Department Annual Report, 1926* (Nairobi: Government Printer), p. 19.

34. Kenya Colony and Protectorate, *Education Department Annual Report, 1949* (Nairobi: Government Printer), p. 3.

35. Kenya Colony and Protectorate, *Education Department Annual Report, 1926* (Nairobi: Government Printer), p. 17.

36. E. W. Smith, *The Christian Mission in Africa* (London: Edinburgh House Press, 1926), p. 110.

37. Kenya Colony and Protectorate, *Education Department Annual Report, 1929* (Nairobi: Government Printer), pp. 16-18. It was decided that the local vernacular should be used as the medium of instruction at first, but (following the policy laid down in a 1927 memorandum, *Future Policy in Africa,* Cmd. 2904) English should be introduced as soon as possible.

38. Oliver, *op. cit.*, pp. 278-283. See also James W. C. Dougall, *Missionary Education in Kenya and Uganda, A Study of Cooperation* (London: International Missionary Council, 1936).

39. John E. Anderson, *The Struggle for the School* (Longmans, 1970); also "Self-Help and Independency: The Political Implications of a Continuing Tradition in African Education in Kenya," *African Affairs,* LXX, no. 278 (January, 1971).

40. Despite such severe racial disparities, the Phelps-Stokes report noted the paradox that African education received more expenditure per capita in territories with large expatriate communities because more funds were generated in agriculture and commerce, and the demand for labor led to more schools. *Phelps-Stokes Reports, op. cit.,* pp. 116, 117.

41. Kenya Colony and Protectorate, *Education Department Annual Report, 1926* (Nairobi: Government Printer), pp. 17, 33.

42. *Ibid.,* p. 13.

43. *Ibid.,* p. 15.

44. *Ibid.,* p. 17.

45. *Ibid.,* p. 13.

46. For a description of the role of the Jeanes teacher see James W. C. Dougall, (ed.), *A Village Teacher's Guide, A Book of Guidance for African Teachers,* compiled by members of the staff of the Jeanes School, Kabete, Kenya (London: The Sheldon Press, 1931); T. G. Benson, "The Jeanes School and the Education of the East African Native," *Journal of the Royal African Society,* XXV, no. 141, (October, 1936), 418-31; J. C. Porter, "Adult Education at the Jeanes School for Community Development in Kenya," *Yearbook of Education, 1954* (London: Evans Brothers Ltd., 1954), pp. 351-356. See also Jeanes Conference, *op. cit.*

47. See T. W. Wallbank, "British Colonial Policy and Native Education in Kenya," *Journal of Negro Education,* VII, no. 4, (October, 1938), 521-32.

48. L. J. Lewis praises the Jeanes Movement in Kenya as one of the most realistic experiments in adapting to changing needs in *Educational Policy and Practice in British Tropical Areas* (London: Nelson and Sons Ltd., 1954), p. 71. See also Richard Heyman, "The Role of the Carnegie Corporation in African Education 1925-1960" (Ed.D. dissertation, Teachers College, 1969).

49. Kenya Colony and Protectorate, *Education Department Annual Report, 1926,* (Nairobi: Government Printer), p. 14.

50. *Ibid.,* p. 25.

51. *Ibid.,* p. 14.

52. *Ibid.,* p. 29. See also R. L. Buell, *The Native Problem in Africa* (London: McMillan, 1928), I, 389.

53. Great Britain Colonial Office, *Memorandum on the Education of African Communities,* Col. no. 103 (H.M.S.O., 1935) (The 1935 Memorandum).

54. L. J. Lewis, *Educational Policy and Practice in British Tropical Areas,* p. 71.

55. Great Britain Colonial Office, *Memorandum on Mass Education in African Society,* Col. no. 186 (London: H.M.S.O., 1943).

56. James J. Shields, Jr., *The Reports of the Phelps-Stokes Fund on Education in Africa and the Formation of a Theory of Community Development by the British* (New York: Phelps-Stokes Fund Occasional Papers no. 4, May 4, 1961), p. 2; see also L. J. Lewis (ed.), *Perspectives in Mass Education and Community Development* (London: Thos. Nelson and Sons, Ltd., 1955) and Lionel Elvin, "Education and Community Development: Some Recent Trends in Africa," *Fundamental and Adult Education,* IX, no. 2 (April, 1957), 59-62.

57. See Ali Mazrui, "European Exploration and Africa's Self-Discovery," *Journal of Modern African Studies,* VII, no. 4 (1969), 661-676.

58. Cohen, *British Policy in Changing Africa,* pp. 22-23.

59. Quoted in G. C. Latham, "Indirect Rule and Education in East Africa," *Africa,* VII, no. 4 (October, 1934), 423.

60. *Ibid.,* p. 424.

61. John Goldthorpe, *Outlines of East African Society* (Kampala: Department of Sociology, Makerere University College, 1959), p. 64. For analyses of various East African tribes see Lloyd Fallers, *Bantu Bureaucracy* (Cambridge: Heffer, 1955) and A. I. Richards, (ed.), *East African Chiefs* (London: Faber and Faber, 1960), both published for the East African Institute of Social Research.

62. Quoted in G. H. Mungeam, *British Rule in Kenya, 1895-1929: The Establishment of Administration* (London: Clarendon Press, 1960), p. 42.

63. Cohen, *op. cit.,* p. 26.

64. T. Ranger, "African Attempts to Control Education in East and Central Africa 1900-1939," *Past and Present,* XXXII (December, 1965), 57-85. See also *Emerging Themes in African History* (Nairobi: East African Publishing House, 1968) and *Aspects of Central African History* (London: Heinemann, 1968).

65. For an excellent analysis of the development of African nationalism in Kenya see Rosberg and Nottingham, *op. cit.*

66. Latham, *op. cit.,* pp. 425-427. See also Sir James Currie and others, "Indirect Rule in Africa and its Bearings on Educational Development," *Oversea Education,* IV, no. 2 (January, 1933), 82-84.

67. Kenya Colony and Protectorate, *Native Administration Department Annual Report, 1926* (Nairobi: Government Printer), p. 23.

68. W. E. F. Ward, "The Beecher Report on African Education in Kenya," *Oversea Education,* XXIV, no. 4 (January, 1953), 13, and Kenya Colony Protectorate, *Education Department Annual Report, 1947* (Nairobi: Government Printer), p. 3.

69. Ingham, *A History of East Africa,* pp. 279-281. See also *Harry Thuku, An Autobiography* (Nairobi: Oxford University Press, 1970).

70. Rosberg and Nottingham, *op. cit.,* pp. 47-53.

71. G. Bennett, "The Development of Political Organizations in Kenya," *Political Studies,* V, no. 2 (June, 1957), 119-122.

72. Ingham, *op. cit.,* p. 282.

73. *Ibid.,* p. 283.

74. For a detailed account of the development of African political participation see Rosberg and Nottingham, *op. cit.,* pp. 35-104.

75. Ingham, *op. cit.,* p. 285.

76. Kenya Colony and Protectorate, *Education Annual Report, 1953* (Nairobi: Government Printer), p. 25.

77. Education was perhaps a more explicit goal of cultural nationalism in Kenya than in other countries, but independent churches have been a remarkably widespread phenomenon throughout sub-Saharan Africa. See David B. Barrett, *Schism and Renewal in Africa: An Analysis of Six Thousand Contemporary Religious Movements* (Nairobi: Oxford University Press, 1968).

78. F. B. Welbourn, *East African Rebels: A Study of Some Independent Churches* (London: S.C.M. Press, 1961), p. 78.

79. *Ibid.,* p. 141.

80. *Ibid.,* p. 154.

81. *Ibid.,* p. 130.

82. Rosberg and Nottingham, *op. cit.,* pp. 105-135.

83. *Ibid.,* pp. 105-135.

84. Welbourn, *op. cit.,* p. 142. Also Jeanes Conference, p. 48.

85. Kenya Colony and Protectorate, *Education Department Annual Report, 1929* (Nairobi: Government Printer), pp. 8, 29.

86. Lord Hailey, *An African Survey: Revised 1956* (London: Oxford University Press, 1957), p. 1168.

87. Welbourn, *op. cit.,* p. 159.

88. L. J. Lewis, *Educational Policy and Practice in British Tropical Areas* (London: Nelson and Sons, Ltd., 1954), p. 5.

89. Kenya Colony and Protectorate, *Education Department Annual Report, 1934* (Nairobi: Government Printer, 1935), p. 9.

90. Kenya Colony and Protectorate, *Education Department Annual Report, 1936* (Nairobi: Government Printer, 1937), p. 102.

91. *Ibid.,* p. 54.

92. Rosberg and Nottingham, *op. cit.,* p. 251. For a detailed analysis of the Kikuyu Independent Schools Movement see Donald Bruce Franklin, "The Kikuyu Independent School: A Study of Response by the Colonial Government in Kenya" (Master's thesis, Teachers College, Columbia University, 1967).

93. T. W. Wallbank, "British Colonial Policy and Native Education in Kenya," *Journal of Negro Education,* VII, no. 4 (October, 1938), 529.

94. "Christian Missionary Education Policy in East Africa," *Oversea Education,* XII, no. 2 (January, 1914), 84-86.

95. Great Britain Colonial Office, *Higher Education in East Africa,* Col. no. 142 (London: H.M.S.O., 1937) (The de la Warr Commission).

96. Arthur Mayhew, *Education in the Colonial Empire* (London: Longmans, 1938), p. 176.

97. See "Report of the Commission on Higher Education in East Africa: A Summary of Its Conclusions," *Oversea Education,* IX, no. 2 (March, 1938), 57-64.

98. Great Britain Colonial Office, *A Survey of Vocational Technical Education in the Colonial Empire,* Col. no. 177 (London: H.M.S.O., 1940).

99. Great Britain Colonial Office, *Report of the Commission on Higher Education in the Colonies,* Cmd. 6647 (London: H.M.S.O., 1945) (The Asquith Commission).

100. Lewis, *Educational Policy and Practice in British Tropical Areas,* pp. 33-39.

101. Hailey, *op. cit.,* p. 193.

102. Great Britain Colonial Office, Advisory Committee for Education in the Colonies, *Education for Citizenship,* Col. no. 216 (London: H.M.S.O., 1948).

103. Kenya Colony and Protectorate, *African Education in Kenya* (Nairobi: Government Printer, 1949), p. 9. Cited hereafter as the Beecher Report.

104. W. E. F. Ward, "The Beecher Report on African Education in Kenya," *Oversea Education,* XXIV, no. 4 (January, 1953), 14.

105. Kenya Colony and Protectorate, *Education Department Annual Report, 1947* (Nairobi: Government Printer), p. 4.

106. Kenya Colony and Protectorate, *Education Department Annual Report, 1949* (Nairobi: Government Printer), p. 64. Unaided schools did not receive government subsidies or "grants-in-aid."

107. *Ibid.,* p. 30.

108. *Ibid.,* pp. 9, 15, 28.

109. *Ibid.,* p. 30.

110. Kenya Colony and Protectorate, *A Ten-Year Plan for the Development of African Education* (Nairobi: Government Printer, 1948).

111. *Ibid.,* pp. 2, 16.

112. Kenya Colony and Protectorate, *Education Department Annual Report, 1949* (Nairobi: Government Printer), p. 5.

113. *Ibid.,* p. 15.

114. *Ibid.,* p. 16.

115. The Committee's full membership included: The Venerable Archdeacon L. J. Beecher (Chairman), the Rev. W. Scott Dickson, Mr. N. B. Larby, the Hon. E. W. Mathu, Mr. D. O'Hagan, Mr. W. Padley, the Rev. Father Rowlands, the Hon. Lady Shaw, with Lt.-Col. F. E. Firminger as Secretary.

CHAPTER III

Education for Colonial Development: 1945-55

THE BEECHER REPORT

The critical situation resulting from the colony's inability to finance the recommendations of the Ten-Year Plan and the Salaries Commission imbued the Beecher Committee's activities with a sense of urgency. Before turning to the specific recommendations of its Report, however, it may be useful to examine some of the conclusions of Beecher's historical review of African education. Referring to the long-standing cooperation between the Government and the missions, Beecher remarked that "the history of the development of African education is largely a history of the development of the grant-in-aid system (1)." Within the Kenya context, this was an accurate assessment of the situation, for the budgetary constraints of the settler-based economy were certainly a primary determinant of the provision of African education.

The most serious problem of the system identified by the Beecher Committee was expansion at the primary level without adequate financial provision or control. Supervision, teacher training, and other aspects of planned development had failed to keep pace with the expansion. In Beecher's words, the system was "a tightly closed vicious circle in which . . . everything expands except control (2)." Beecher himself recognized that the intense pressures being brought to bear upon the missions and Government had increased the quantity of educational facilities at the expense of quality. In order to reverse this trend strict supervision was necessary to control primary school expansion, while expansion at the secondary and teacher training levels was expected to restore some semblance of balance to the system (3). Thus, the Beecher Committee chose to break the vicious circle through financial control of primary education.

Some Africans interpreted the emphasis on control as an indication of the Government's intention to take over the independent schools (4). However, despite the emphasis on increasing the inspectorial and supervisory staff (5) which appeared to centralize the system, Beecher repeatedly stressed the importance of sustaining local initiative.

To ease the financial burden on local authorities, the Beecher Report recommended that responsibility for primary and intermediate schools be placed under reconstituted District Education Boards. Four Regional Education Boards would be responsible for municipalities, primary and intermediate schools outside the Native Land Units, girls' intermediate schools, and all secondary schools and teacher training institutions (6). To ensure local participation under the Regional Education Boards, Boards of Governors would be appointed to supervise the implementation of policy in each school. However, the most discussed—perhaps because it was the most obvious—change brought about by the Beecher Report was the introduction of a 4-4-4 system of primary, intermediate, and secondary schools to replace the previous 6-2-4 organization.

Despite these administrative changes, the Beecher Report essentially reaffirmed the basic objectives of African education which had evolved prior to 1948. The Committee's first recommendation stressed the importance of maintaining cooperation between the Government and the voluntary agencies as a basis for teaching "Christian principles." In asserting the necessity for a religion-based education and the continued use of the grant-in-aid system, the Report quoted passages from the 1925 Memorandum as proof of the continuity of educational policy. But in an important break with the past, it stated that independent schools would be considered "voluntary agencies," thus qualifying them for aid (7). Another carry-over from the 1925 Memorandum was the idea that education should meet the needs of a predominantly rural society. Thus, the Report reiterated a common theme which ultimately led to the Conference on Education, Employment and Rural Development, held at Kericho in 1966 (8). Realizing that Africans generally preferred literary to "practical" education, the Committee took great pains to cite evidence in defense of its position (9), determining the territory's general manpower requirements in commercial, technical, and other fields and calculating the number of children capable of receiving various levels of education. Both these arguments were based on insubstantial empirical evidence.

Any estimates of Kenya's manpower requirements had to be made within the context of the racially stratified economy, in which most of the high-level jobs were reserved for Europeans. Thus, there was little demand for Africans with more than a primary education (10). In illustration of the growth of scientific testing and measurement since the 1925 Memorandum, the Beecher Report included graphs on the "Distribution and Relations of Educational Abilities," which indicated that of the 10,000 African children in Kenya between the ages of seven and 11 attending primary school, less than 23 percent were "suitable for education beyond the primary stage (11)." Such calculations seem extraordinarily naive in view of recent research, which has cast severe doubts on the establishment of any limits of this sort by early testing, and they rather suspiciously complement the racial dogma underlying colonialism.

Taking wastage into account, Beecher applied these calculations to the Kenya situation and recommended the following pattern of development, shown in contrast with the proposals of the Ten-Year Plan (12):

Standard (grade)	1948 Enrollment	1957 on Ten-Year Plan	1957 on Beecher Plan
1	113,987	60,000	180,000
2	51,160	60,000	110,000
3	36,849	60,000	70,000
4	26,018	60,000	60,000
5	21,578	40,000	13,600
6	6,983	40,000	13,600
7	3,046	4,200	11,050
8	2,204	4,200	11,050
Form			
I	278	800	960
II	194	800	960
III	57	400	480
IV	39	400	480

It is evident that the Beecher Report was more realistic—or pessimistic—than the Ten-Year Plan concerning wastage in the early years. The figures also reveal Beecher's determination to treat each level—primary, intermediate, and secondary—as having educational value in itself. Beecher replaced the Ten-Year Plan's goal of six years of education for half the territory's children with one of providing, by 1961, four years of primary schooling for all who wanted it. One writer described Beecher's plan as a "definite attempt to design a pattern of education that would keep the majority of primary leavers in the rural areas (13)." Allowing for a continued, if not increasing, high rate of wastage, Beecher also recommended the elimination of "unjustifiable promotion, and the retention of 'repeaters' in any given standard after they have reached their educational ceiling (14)." When taken together with the Committee's recommendations for improving the teaching profession (15), the overall effect was the substitution of qualitative control for quantitative expansion as the primary force behind African education.

Reaction to the Beecher Report

The closing paragraphs of the Beecher Report made a plea for the immediate recruitment of European staff, even before the plan itself was to go into effect (16). The sense of urgency was so great that instead of advertising through the usual channels, the Kenya Government printed a brochure describing the attractions of working in Kenya and sent several

education officers to Britain to recruit teachers. These efforts yielded
dividends, and the arrival of additional staff prompted one observer to remark
that "for the first time in its history, the Kenya Education Department has
the men it needs to do the job (17)."

Shortly thereafter, the Advisory Council on African Education enthusiastically endorsed the Beecher Report as providing:

for the first time a clear statement of African educational policy in Kenya,
and, if this is carried out with determination, we can look forward to a period
of rapid progress and improvement in the educational system which will have
a far-reaching effect on the country's development in general (18).

After a three-day debate, the Legislative Council approved the Beecher
Report in August, 1950, and the Government soon began the task of
reorganization (19). The Member for Education, Health and Local Government issued a statement on the Government's program of implementation in
which he recognized the importance of reviewing the policy periodically,
rather than allowing it to become static (20).

Unfortunately, however, educational policy received little attention in
Kenya during the 1950's, for a number of reasons. As a result of this neglect,
the Beecher Report, according to a prominent headmaster in Kenya, was
"used far beyond its own schedule and therefore comes under criticism which
it hardly deserved (21)." In contrast to the Government's enthusiasm,
Africans were highly critical of the Report, and its ultimate impact must be
seen from the African point of view. Their objections fell mainly into two
categories: the first was the complaint that Beecher's emphasis on quality
rather than quantity meant that enrollment would grow too slowly, thus
frustrating African hopes for universal literacy; the second criticism was
directed against the replacement of the 6-2-4 system by the 4-4-4 system.
Many Africans argued that the four-year primary school course would be too
short to achieve permanent literacy, and that too few students would get
beyond the fourth grade to make the intermediate level worthwhile (22). One
African writer recalled that education ranked with land, freedom, and wages
as the key points of dispute between Africans and Europeans. These issues
were voiced by Jomo Kenyatta in a speech in July, 1952, just three months
before the declaration of the State of Emergency (23).

Despite such criticisms, there can be no doubt of the importance of the
Beecher Report. Not only was it the only comprehensive survey of African
education in Kenya before Independence but, unlike most reports, it was
formally approved and acted upon. Before analyzing the implications of the
Beecher Report within the framework of overall colonial policy, it will be
useful to examine other surveys and proposals made concerning education
during the period 1945-55.

THE BINNS REPORT AND THE CAMBRIDGE CONFERENCE

The Cambridge Conference, described by its chairman, Sir Philip Morris, as the first thorough survey of the "whole groundwork of education in colonial territories" since the Phelps Stokes Reports and the 1925 Memorandum (24), was held from September 8 to September 20, 1952, under the joint auspices of the Nuffield Foundation and the Colonial Office. The decision to hold a conference attended by a broad cross section of Africans and Europeans concerned with colonial education, rather than send out a more formal commission, was based on the idea that all those involved in the educational process should share in the formulation of policy (25). This recognition preceded Kenya's independence by ten years, and marked the beginning of a movement toward African representation and participation in policy discussions.

The procedures agreed upon were for "small groups of experts" to visit Britain's African territories prior to the Conference, and to prepare reports which would be used as a basis for discussion at the Conference itself. The groups were appointed in March, 1951, and spent the last six months of the year in Africa. Dr. G. B. Jeffery led the West Africa group, while A. L. Binns was chairman of the East and Central Africa study group. Binns, who had been Chief Education Officer for the Lancashire County Council, was accompanied by Professor B. A. Fletcher, the Director of the Institute of Education at Bristol University, and Miss F. W. Gwilliam, Assistant Education Adviser to the Secretary of State; even in 1952 no African was appointed to such a panel.

Several aspects of the Report, which contained 76 recommendations in all, have particular relevance to the evolution of educational policy in Kenya (26). Covering a wide variety of territories and reflecting the authorship of "outsiders"—as compared with Beecher's long acquaintance with Kenya—the Binns Report at first glance appears too general to have specific relevance for Kenya. In a sense, however, this broader perspective enabled the Binns group to place Kenya within the historical framework of a rapidly changing continent, while Beecher's closeness to the situation had kept him from obtaining an overview of it.

The differences in the changes advocated by the two reports were less a matter of content than of degree. For example, both reports advocated a tightening of the supervisory and inspectorial system while encouraging local initiative through the growth of governing boards for most schools. The Binns Report, however, advocated even more centralized control than Beecher had recommended, and specifically criticized the Beecher Plan for leaving missionaries largely responsible for the supervision of mission schools (27). The Binns Report went on to recommend that representatives of both church and Government schools be included on all governing boards (28), in preparation for the eventual unification of the schools. This centralization of control did not imply that education was to become secularized, however. Binns stressed "the deep-rooted belief that religion must be the basis of education [and that] intellectual advancement, as evinced by good examination results, achieved at the expense of sound moral and cultural growth, will not suffice (29)."

The concern of the Binns Report with the "disintegration of tribal morals" not only led it to insist upon a religious basis for education, but also shaped its language policy. The Report strongly recommended preserving selected tribal vernaculars, while advocating the general elimination of Swahili, except where it was the local vernacular—reasoning that its use as a lingua franca impeded the learning of both the vernacular and English. The authors of the Report contended, "To preserve the vernacular languages of Africa is to preserve the tribes that speak them and to strengthen the moral sanctions that rest on tribal membership (30)."

In advocating four years of teaching in the vernacular, Binns was in full agreement with the Beecher Report, and recommended that Beecher's 4-4-4 plan be followed in other territories (31). Where Beecher had not recommended formal teaching of agriculture below the intermediate level (32), Binns advocated using the primary school as the focus for agricultural training, because agriculture would remain the livelihood of most Africans and too few students progressed beyond the primary level to benefit from more advanced training (33). Binns did not expect primary school students to master a full repertoire of agricultural skills; he merely hoped to establish the proper attitudes at an early age.

Binns agreed with Beecher in looking to the teacher training colleges as the principal means of improving the quality of the primary and intermediate schools, but he went further than Beecher in stressing Africanization of the teacher training institutions, both in hiring more African instructors (34) and in fitting the curriculum more closely to the practical realities of the African environment. In language reminiscent of the 1925 Memorandum, Binns called for a curriculum suited to African rather than European needs (35).

The Binns Report offered specific recommendations on such long-standing problems as women's education, urban areas, boarding schools, and technical education. Few of the proposals marked significant advances in policy (36), but in the field of adult education the Binns Report gave new hope for achieving the goals identified in the 1935 *Memorandum on the Education of African Communities* and in the 1944 *Memorandum on Mass Education in African Societies.* Binns suggested the use of films on agricultural techniques and the establishment of camps to offer short courses for teachers, modeled on the Scandinavian Folk High Schools. Noting that adult education was usually the responsibility of the Department of Social

Welfare, he recommended that it be placed under the Department of Education and treated as a follow-up to primary education (37).

On matters of finance, Binns essentially agreed with the Beecher Report, but urged that an effort be made to see that certain individuals or districts were not burdened unfairly (38). Pointing to the failure of the Beecher Plan, as implemented, "to distinguish between the need of one area and another," Binns advocated that the remission or reduction of fees be the responsibility of the District Commissioners, and eventually of the African local authorities (39).

Binns and his colleagues expressed shock that the Beecher Report accepted a wastage of 50 percent during primary school, and implied that the problem of wastage would essentially be solved if their own recommendations were accepted (40). The history of education throughout the African continent indicates that wastage is extremely difficult to eliminate, but while Beecher's calculations may have been more realistic, Binns was correct in noting that rate of wastage between primary and intermediate school in Kenya was exceptionally severe (41).

Of far greater importance than the actual numbers or percentages of the population enrolled in schools was the recognition that the planning of educational development must be closely integrated with overall territorial development. Binns was well aware of the economic implications of keeping educational policy in step with developments in various occupations, in order to achieve maximum productivity with a minimum of frustration and unemployment. Since they believed that the economic development of Kenya would for some time to come be based upon agricultural production, the Binns Report advocated directing education towards increasing the productivity of the rural sector, thus reiterating the need for a rural orientation in education (42).

The Cambridge Conference Proceedings

Using the Binns Report on East and Central Africa and the Jeffery Report on West Africa as a basis for discussion, the Cambridge Conference divided itself into five working groups, each studying one aspect of African education: responsibility and control; the expansion of the educational system; the teaching profession; organization and the curriculum; and education and the adult.

Although the editor of the Conference's report, W. E. F. Ward of the Colonial Office, indicated the degree to which the speakers were agreed on various points, it was clear that "the purpose of the conference was not to make policy . . . [but] to place on record the best views which could be formalized and expressed" for the use of those responsible for planning and carrying out educational developments.

The group concerned with responsibility and control affirmed the necessity of continuing cooperation between the voluntary agencies and the central or local Government authorities. Local authorities were to take the main responsibility for primary and intermediate schools, and the central Government for secondary and higher education (43).

Although the expansion of the educational system was generally felt to be the "most politically exciting" of the five topics (44), the line of discussion followed by that group, and later the full Conference, was essentially conservative. Although the group identified many of the long-standing problems in African education, such as women's education and wastage, they merely endorsed the efforts that were already being made, such as improving teacher quality, rather than suggesting new approaches (45). It is significant that when a working group did take a somewhat progressive position, for example, advocating the allocation of a larger proportion of the national budget for education, the Conference as a whole did not go along, but indicated the more conservative nature of their thinking (46).

In the group concerned with the teaching profession, there was general agreement that the upgrading of that profession was basic to the improvement of the educational system as a whole, and the group agreed with the Binns Report that institutes of education be set up. Despite the consensus that universities should play a larger role in training teachers and in conducting research, there was disagreement regarding the best means of accomplishing this. Some advocated using British institutes of education as the model, while others pointed to American teacher training institutions as a type that might successfully be adapted to African conditions (47).

In discussing the issues involved in organization and curriculum, the group studying those questions noted the general African opposition to Beecher's 4-4-4 plan. To determine the most appropriate organizational pattern for a Kenyan school system, the working group identified three areas which they felt should be given balanced consideration in every territory during the planning stages of the new system: (a) what was educationally desirable; (b) what the people of the country desired (a factor which had been minimized in many previous cases); (c) what was financially possible (48). All members of the group concerned with organizational patterns agreed that the process by which students were selected to proceed beyond a certain level was a basic issue of proposed change. Among their suggestions for improving this process, the group recommended the use of school records and interviews to avoid overreliance on examination results (49). In marked contrast to Beecher and Binns, the same group de-emphasized the use of the tribal languages and urged more teaching in English in the primary schools (50). But in tackling such difficult problems as the improvement of agricultural techniques or race relations, they, like most of their peers, stressed that progress would be achieved not merely by verbalizing ideals, but by demonstration and actual practice (51).

Perhaps the most significant direction taken by the Cambridge Conference was its emphasis on adult education. Although there was disagreement over whether the work of adult education or community development could best be carried out in a separate department or within the Ministry of Education, the work group on adult education agreed that informal education must be closely coordinated with formal schooling (52). It distinguished between literacy campaigns and general community development, and went on to recommend that "at least for the short-term there should be quite novel concentration of energy and resources upon the tasks of informal education (53)." Since numerous speakers endorsed this proposal and none opposed it, W. E. F. Ward concluded that it was "certainly the most revolutionary sentence spoken during the conference (54)." If the colonial governments had in fact placed such a high priority upon informal education, the effect upon the African continent would have been truly revolutionary. However, despite the enthusiasm expressed for adult education, the proposal failed to be implemented to any significant degree because of the difficulty of reallocating resources from formal education.

In evaluating the importance of the conference, Sir Philip Morris stated in the epilogue to its Report that:

The success of the Cambridge Conference cannot now be assessed; its measure will in due course be what peoples and the Governments of British territories in Africa, partly because of it, find themselves able to decide upon and carry into effect (55).

A CRITICAL SUMMARY

As mentioned in Chapter II, the Colonial Development and Welfare Act of 1945 was a sharp departure from the previous policy of colonial self-sufficiency. The Beecher Report and Cambridge Conference indicated that Britain had decided to play a more positive role in African education, as well as in more general areas. With reference to this Act and its 1940 predecessor, Sir Andrew Cohen, the Secretary of State for the Colonies, described the "new look" that British colonial policy acquired during the Second World War (56). Besides the decision to develop colonial dependencies financially, the new approach revealed itself in a new policy of local government and in constitutional changes. As enunciated in 1947, the policy of local government "aimed at converting the system of indirect rule into an efficient, representative and modern system of local government," and the policy of constitutional advance involved bringing Africans into the Legislative Council and extending the popular suffrage (57). At the time, Kenya lagged far behind many other British African territories in the area of political progress toward majority rule. However, the home Government's more positive approach to the political and economic development of the colonies marked a significant shift from Britain's former policy of trusteeship. Rather than merely responding to the initiatives shown by the various governors, the Colonial Office after the war became an active force in the formation of policy (58).

The most serious miscalculation in colonial policy immediately after the war was the assumption that the colonial system would continue for an indefinite period, but there was a growing realization in most quarters during the 1950's that many elements of that system were inherently unstable. It is not clear, however, whether the policy makers were fully aware of the revolutionary impact of the constitutional changes and dramatic expansion of education, developments which further stimulated the Africans' demands for control over their destiny.

Despite several statements in the Beecher and Binns Reports that education could accelerate overall development if it were given a higher priority in territorial budgets, the planning and implementation of educational policy remained isolated to a great extent from developments in other areas of government. Perhaps the most striking weakness of educational policy making in the post-war era of colonial development was the educators' naïveté concerning social and political forces alien to them. Beecher, for example, underestimated the growing intensity of the Africans' demands for educational opportunity, while Binns' nostalgic endorsement of vernacular languages as a means of building up the tribes' moral institutions was tragically inappropriate.

The result of these weaknesses was an interpretation of education for colonial development as a policy devoted to patching up the most obvious defects in the existing system, such as wastage and the low proportion of girls enrolled in school. If the framework within which African education functioned had remained fairly stable, the policies recommended by Beecher and Binns might have brought about better supervision and control, and thus improved the quality of education. But the colonial framework was far from static, and this approach to educational policy making never really had a chance, for in looking inward at ways to improve the system, educators had failed to take account of outside forces that would place new burdens upon educational systems. Education for colonial development failed because during the 1950's the very basis of colonialism was undermined by the growth of African nationalism.

Notes

1. Beecher Report, p. v.

2. *Ibid.*, p. 12. It is interesting that Beecher places the blame for the secondary bottleneck on an excess of local enthusiasm for primary education rather than on the Government's failure to expand secondary education.

3. For summaries Beecher Report; pp. vii, viii, and "African Education in Kenya: The Beecher Report," *Times Educational Supplement* (London), no. 1852, October 27, 1950, p. 821.

4. Karuri Njama and Donald L. Barnett, *Mau Mau From Within* (New York: Monthly Review, 1967), pp. 77, 78. Also George Bennett, *Kenya: A Political History*.

5. Chapter five of the Report deals with the recruitment and training of additional European staff. It is likely that the term European in this sense refers to qualified personnel rather than connoting racial bias. This interpretation is borne out by the Beecher Report's later concern with the upgrading of African staff.

6. See Beecher Report, pp. 95-97, for a full explanation of these administrative changes.

7. *Ibid.*, p. 51.

8. *Ibid.*, p. vii. See Chapter VI of this book for a discussion of the Kericho Conference.

9. *Ibid.*, pp. 27-32.

10. See Sheldon Weeks, *Divergence in Educational Development: The Case of Kenya and Uganda* (New York: Teachers College Press, 1967), p. 7.

11. Beecher Report, pp. 68, 69.

12. Ward, "The Beecher Report on African Education in Kenya," p. 18.

13. Weeks, *op. cit.,* p. 6.

14. Beecher Report, p. 71.

15. *Ibid.*, pp. 81-86.

16. *Ibid.*, p. 141.

17. Ward, "The Beecher Report on African Education in Kenya," p. 19.

18. Kenya Colony and Protectorate, Sessional Paper No. 1 of 1950, *Proposals for the Implementation of the Recommendations of the Report on African Education in Kenya* (Nairobi: Government Printer, 1950), p. 26.

19. Kenya Colony and Protectorate, *Education Department Annual Report, 1950* (Nairobi: Government Printer), p. 5.

20. *Ibid.*, p. 43.

21. L. J. Campbell, Headmaster of Alliance High School, Kikuyu, Kenya, letter to author, dated December 16, 1963. See also Ward, "The Beecher Report on Education in Kenya," p. 13.

22. Ward, "The Beecher Report on African Education in Kenya," p. 19.

23. Njama and Barnett, *op. cit.,* p. 77. Njama states emphatically that most Africans viewed the Beecher Report as a deliberate attempt on the part of Government to hold back African development by restricting education of all but a tiny fraction to a mere four years of school.

24. Nuffield Foundation and Colonial Office, *African Education: A Study of Educational Policy and Practice in British Tropical Areas* (Oxford: Oxford University Press, 1953), p. ix. Hereafter referred to as the Cambridge Conference.

25. *Ibid.*, pp. ix-xi.

26. See Binns Report, pp. 134-140. Binns also wrote a brief article, "The Education of Africans in East and Central Africa," *Colonial Review*, VII (December, 1952), 232-235, which summarizes many of the group's findings.

27. Binns Report, p. 65. Binns' criticism of Beecher was tempered during the Conference proceedings. See Cambridge Conference, p. 147.

28. *Ibid.*, p. 67.

28. *Ibid.*, p. 68.

30. *Ibid.*, pp. 80-81.

31. *Ibid.*, pp. 74, 80.

32. Beecher Report, pp. 63, 71.

33. Binns Report, pp. 65-70, 98-100.

34. The Binns Report defined the ideal school as "interracial," p. 68.

35. *Ibid.*, p. 67.

36. For the detailed analysis of these issues see *Ibid.*, chapters 18, 22, 21, and 14 respectively.

37. *Ibid.*, pp. 102-106.

38. For the details of the financial recommendations see *Ibid.*, pp. 131-133.

39. *Ibid.*, p. 127.

40. *Ibid.*, pp. 77-79.

41. According to the Binns Report, Kenya had 31.2 percent of the age groups in schools for four years, 3.7 percent for eight years, and 0.8 percent for 12 years in 1950, pp. 75, 76.

42. Cambridge Conference, p. 142.

43. *Ibid.*, p. 143.

44. *Ibid.*, p. 151.

45. For specific examples see *Ibid.*, pp. 151-155.

46. I am using the term "progressive" here in the sense of forward-thinking or anticipatory (gained with the benefit of hindsight), while "conservative" refers to the preference to keep the present system with minor alterations.

47. Cambridge Conference, pp. 163-165.

48. *Ibid.*, p. 168.

49. *Ibid.*, pp. 166, 170.

50. *Ibid.*, pp. 166, 170.

51. *Ibid.*, pp. 166, 170, 173.

52. The Report's editor noted the confusion resulting from the various names applied to adult education, such as mass education, informal education, community development, and fundamental education. Cambridge Conference, p. 176.

53. *Ibid.*, p. 177.

54. *Ibid.*, p. 177.

55. *Ibid.*, p. 183. For a useful, brief survey of the Cambridge Conference see John McLeod Campbell, *African History in the Making* (London: Edinburgh House Press, 1956).

56. Cohen, *op. cit.*, p. 131.

57. *Ibid.*, p. 33.

58. *Ibid.*, pp. 82-84.

CHAPTER IV

Winds of Change

THE NEW COLONIAL PERSPECTIVE

During the 1950's and early 1960's the African continent reverberated with a series of profound changes which marked the end of most of the colonial empires. Although Prime Minister MacMillan's reference in a speech at Cape Town to the "winds of change" fell upon deaf ears in southern Africa, Great Britain responded to the mounting pressures of nationalism by granting self-government and eventual independence to her colonial dependencies in a series of progressive stages (1). In Kenya, because of the entrenched opposition of the settler community, and related problems among the Africans, the attainment of independence was slower and more complex than in most of the other territories. Rather than repeat general material ably presented elsewhere (2), this chapter analyzes the changing political, social, and economic framework within which education in Kenya was shaped.

In examining what Margery Perham has called "the colonial reckoning," the most difficult task facing historians is to distinguish between what was given up by Britain with reluctant benevolence, and what was taken by Africans as a result of their own initiatives. Complex forces within postwar Kenya caused Great Britain to alter its fundamental relationship with the colony and to accelerate the pace of political change dramatically (3).

The achievement of independence in India and other countries in Asia, and the international forum provided after 1945 by the United Nations, had a profound effect on world opinion. No longer could the fortunes of Africans in Kenya depend merely upon bilateral discussion between the settlers and the British Government. During the 1950's the growth of nationalism in West Africa and the increasing commitment of African nationalists to Pan-African unity lent further support to the winds of change in Kenya.

The Second World War heralded a new period of militant political nationalism in Kenya, replacing the major concern of earlier African associations with obtaining redress of grievances. Yet Sir Philip Mitchell, appointed Governor in 1944, believed that political and social problems could best be approached through economic development. This economic orientation, based on support for increased European participation in Kenya's economy, was more concerned with total production than with adjusting distribution of economic opportunities, and such a scheme had little appeal to Africans.

The return of African World War II veterans increased the already serious problems of urban unemployment and overcrowding in the reserves. As the disparities between European prosperity and African poverty became more pronounced, the incompatibility of African and European aims within a system of economic dualism became increasingly evident. In the years after 1945, African dependence on wage employment increased. In 1952, African agriculture still represented only six percent of Kenya's net production, compared with 63 percent for Uganda. The Kenya African Union (KAU) launched a major land petition in 1951 which revealed a near crisis in economic affairs. Yet the Government chose to treat it as "an irresponsible attempt by an unrepresentative minority to reverse established economic policies and to reopen land issues that had been justly settled (4)." In the postwar period, although faced with growing economic distress among Africans, the colonial administration refused to accept the need for radical changes in its overall policies in order to meet a radically changing environment, despite the fact that influential sections of European opinion had prophesied trouble as early as 1943 (5).

For Africans, the important political question of the postwar years was whether Independence would be won by constitutional means or whether, as many Africans believed, violence would be necessary. Between 1944 and 1952, the number of African representatives in the Legislative Council increased from one to six, but these members continued to be nominated by the Governor rather than elected. When Jomo Kenyatta returned from England and assumed leadership of the KAU in 1947, Governor Mitchell advised him to "make a start in local government," indicating little interest in Kenyatta's qualifications and potential support as a national spokesman for African interests (6). In 1950, Mitchell, reflecting the common paternalistic attitude of the colonial authorities and correctly estimating the level of education available to Africans, maintained that "the poeple whom it is customary to describe in this country as the educated Africans are people with the sort of education that our children have by the time they are twelve years of age (7)." Between 1945 and the beginning of the Emergency in 1952, the KAU failed to achieve the economic and political reforms it had sought by political means, and this failure rapidly led to more violent demands by Africans for self-determination.

THE STATE OF EMERGENCY

The role of the Mau Mau rebellion in Kenyan politics has been the subject of heated controversy. On the one hand, it was officially and widely interpreted in the 1950's and 1960's as a highly sophisticated, centralized organization, ruthlessly forcing a minority of the Kikuyu tribe to "revert to barbarity" and to forsake all social and political progress (8). On the other hand, revisionist interpretations, such as that of Rosberg and Nottingham, view the movement within the context of the long-term growth of African nationalism (9). This interpretation is supported by most recent observers, who look upon the rebellion as the inevitable result of two conflicting forces: the mounting frustration of the Africans and their continuing repression by the colonial Government.

The membership of the group embraced diverse motivations and goals, and Mau Mau indisputably had a major political impact on British rule in Kenya. The crisis which it generated led to the series of constitutional changes which preceded Independence (10). Whether or not Kenyatta is considered responsible for the growth of the movement, it was evident when he assumed office as Prime Minister in 1963 that popular support for him transcended tribal lines and provided a focal point for national feeling (11).

Kenyatta's conviction for his alleged leadership of the rebellion was based largely on circumstantial evidence and even perjury (12); there is evidence that he actually tried to restrain the movement's more extreme elements (13). Kenyatta's trial was an attempt by the Government to provide justification for the State of Emergency, and a foundation for the official interpretation of Mau Mau. The Government's policy of "rehabilitating" Kikuyu adherents of Mau Mau was based on the assumption of psychological rather than social bases for African political opposition (14). However, Josiah Mwangi Kariuki, a former detainee, described the nationalistic role of Mau Mau as follows: "We do not regard the soldiers of the forest as 'hard-core' terrorists or 'murderers' but as the noblest of our fighters for freedom (15)."

Although the Kikuyu were in the vanguard of political protest, it became clear during the Emergency that their objectives had strong support among leaders of many other ethnic groups. The implementation in 1954 of the Lyttleton Constitution, which made provision for the first time for the election of Africans to the Legislative Council, and the Swynnerton Plan (16), for the intensification of African agriculture, was more than a coincidence. The climate of social discontent and endemic hostility intensified by the Emergency forcibly brought conditions in Kenya to the attention of the British Government and the world at large. The necessity for British military action both confirmed the weakness of the European settlers' position in Kenya and emphasized the increasing financial burden of maintaining colonial rule. African nationalism thus succeeded in the 1950's in creating a new political context in which successive British Colonial Secretaries accepted the urgent need for political and economic change.

POLITICAL WINDS OF CHANGE

The period from the beginning of the Emergency in 1952 until Independence in 1963 saw not only gradual constitutional reform but a measure of reconciliation between the different racial groups in Kenya. Beginning with the creation of African District Councils in 1950, colonial policy in the early 1950's stressed the development of responsible local government. On the national level, although the 1954 Lyttleton Constitution and the 1958 Lennox-Boyd Constitution increased African representation in both the legislative and executive bodies, the British Government continued to adhere to multiracial principles, which meant the continued separation of the major racial groups. The compromise solution which these constitutions contained satisfied none of the racial groups involved. The result was a dogged rear-guard action by the majority of European settlers, who wished to maintain their supremacy, and an increasingly effective policy of noncooperation by the growing number of African political activists.

Although the Government permitted the revival of African political parties in 1955, they remained forbidden on a nationwide level, forcing the surge of nationalism into parochial patterns with an emphasis on local personalities and regional loyalties (17). Only the Kenya Federation of Labor could speak for Africans throughout the Colony; it operated increasingly as a political movement under the able leadership of Tom Mboya. The first African elections in 1957 provided a new constitutional vehicle whereby the nominated African moderates were replaced by a new breed of nationalists, who made clear their opposition to anything less than majority rule.

The critical turning point in Kenya's political progress was the constitutional conference held at Lancaster House in London in 1960, under the chairmanship of Iain MacLeod. After much debate, the conference reached a general agreement, and published a White Paper in February, 1960 (18). Although 20 of the 65 seats for elected members were to be reserved for the immigrant communities, the Africans were assured of a majority on a common voter's roll (19). Soon after the Lancaster House Conference, two African nationalist parties emerged, the Kenya African National Union (KANU) and the Kenya African Democratic Union (KADU). KANU was based mainly on a coalition of Kenya's two largest tribes, the Kikuyu and Luo, while KADU was formed primarily as a reaction against the domination of these tribes (20).

The refusal of the majority party, KANU, to take office without the release from prison of their proclaimed leader, Kenyatta, resulted in a period of instability after the 1961 election. Until Kenyatta's release in 1962, KADU attempted, with some support from the British Government, to rule as a minority party. KADU's concern for finding a way to protect the interests of the minority tribes led to a call for the establishment of a regional constitution (*Majimbo* in Swahili). The ensuing period of bureaucratic confusion had important consequences for education in allowing rapid expansion of self-help schools through local initiative (21). KANU took over as the ruling party in 1963 and has pursued a policy of increased centralization of authority since Independence in December, 1963. Although regional fears and jealousies have not disappeared, KANU's control of rewards and punishment has aided the party in its drive to broaden its support, and during the period of internal self-government, Kenyatta's great popularity and prestige enabled him to "hold the allegiance of most of the militants while also successfully reassuring European farmers and others that they have a worthwhile future in Kenya (22)."

THE NEW ECONOMIC PERSPECTIVE

The Swynnerton Plan of 1954, by stressing the accelerated production of cash crops by Africans (there had been very slight concessions prior to the Swynnerton Plan, modifying the previous ban on African cash crops), symbolized the end of economic dualism in Kenya by giving Africans almost the same farming rights as white settlers (23). A related agricultural problem was the pressing need for land consolidation. Of the basic problems of African economics identified by Sir Andrew Cohen (24), the lack of a system of individual land tenure had been particularly persistent and had discouraged innovation among the primarily subsistence farmers. Understanding little about the customs of land ownership and use which were fundamental aspects of tribal culture, the Government had been largely unsuccessful in its efforts to change the system until the Emergency.

It was the concentration of the Kikuyu, in particular, in villages for security reasons which led to a major reformulation of land boundaries between 1953 and 1955. At the beginning of the Mau Mau acitvity, the Government used land consolidation as a political reward for Kikuyu loyalists, by bringing five or ten small separate plots together so they could be properly surveyed and a deed given to the owner to enable him to get loans. With the reestablishment of law and order in 1956, emphasis shifted to the economic priority of creating a settled peasantry. Productivity increased dramatically, and by establishing individual ownership, the Government was able to establish a framework within which it could provide long-term support in such form as loans, supervision, and marketing facilities (25).

The new importance accorded to African economic development by the Government was reaffirmed by a series of statements proposing that land in the highlands be made available to those Africans capable of meeting certain financial and agricultural requirements (26). The European community saw this as a direct threat to the basis of their existence, and reacted violently. It was not until after the Lancaster House Conference of 1960 that a solution was found to the problem of resettling Africans while keeping land values relatively stable. The Land Scheme that was initiated in 1960 made £14,000,000 available for a three-year development program. The plan, which actually involved five related schemes (27), provided £6,000,000 for land purchase and £8,000,000 for land development resettlement.

More important than the actual programs implementing the new policy toward African agriculture was the new approach to the overall process of development (28). Although education was given high priority in Kenya's 1960 Ten-Year Plan and subsequent development proposals, there had been little effort immediately after the war to utilize education as an integral part of the colonial development program. An interesting example of the reluctance to employ education for African economic development is revealed in the Jeffery Report's statement that "unless it [West Africa] can deploy its manpower to the best advantage, all its schemes for progress and development will come to naught. . . . But these questions are for the economist rather than the educationist (29)."

As soon as it became clear that the African territories were to become independent, educators, together with economists, turned their attention to the enormous challenge of providing sufficient skilled manpower to enable Africans to run their own nations. In Kenya, the problem was particularly difficult because such a high percentage of the territory's wealth was produced by the immigrant races.

The first influential report written from the manpower-planning point of view was the Ashby Report of 1960 (30). As the title, *Investment in Education*, implied, the Commission considered funds allocated to secondary and higher education an investment in the economic development of the nation (31).

IMPLICATIONS FOR EDUCATION

As it became apparent that Kenya was moving towards Independence, educational policy makers were faced with new considerations. Rapid changes in the political structure required the creation of appropriate new economic and social structures. Although the new political and economic demands upon education were closely interrelated, it is possible to distinguish between major concerns. With African political responsibility came the need for national unity and an intensified popular demand for schooling. The Government came under increased pressure to Africanize posts in the civil service and industries by replacing expatriates with Africans. At the same time, there was a growing realization that the skills and capital of expatriates would continue to play a major role in Kenya's economic development for many years to come. Although both economic and political development required large expenditures for the education of Africans equipped to help build the society, the needs of the two areas were not identical. For example, the economy demanded skilled manpower, indicating that secondary and higher education should receive the highest priority, while the general popular demand, expressed at the ballot box, was for universal primary education.

Notes

1. Numerous studies have examined the forces of African nationalism. Rupert Emerson, *From Empire to Nation* (Cambridge: Harvard University Press, 1960) offers a useful analysis of decolonization throughout the Third World. Major studies of the phenomenon in Africa include Thomas Hodgkin, *Nationalism in Colonial Africa* (New York: New York University Press, 1957); George Shepherd, Jr., *The Politics of African Nationalism* (New York: Praeger, 1962); Immanuel Wallerstein, *Africa: The Politics of Independence* (New York: Vintage, 1961); and Margery Perham, *The Colonial Reckoning* (New York: Knopf, 1962).

2. See particularly Rosberg and Nottingham, *The Myth of Mau Mau* and Bennet, *Kenya: A Political History.*

3. Hodgkin, *op. cit.*, p. 9.

4. Rosberg and Nottingham, *op. cit.*, p. 224.

5. Bethwell A. Ogot, "Kenya Under the British, 1895-1963," in Ogot and Kieran (eds.), *Zamani: A Survey of East African History*, pp. 255-289. This is the best short summary of the colonial period.

6. Ingham, *A History of East Africa*, pp. 426-428.

7. Ogot and Kieran, *op. cit.*, p. 283.

8. The official Government study was by F. D. Corfield, entitled *Historical Study of the Origins and Growth of Mau Mau* (London: H.M.S.O., 1960). Dr. J. C. Carothers authored another report, *The Psychology of Mau Mau* (Nairobi: Government Printer, 1954) which reached conclusions similar to Corfield's.

9. Rosberg and Nottingham, *op. cit.*

10. I do not imply direct causality, but it is clear that Mau Mau stimulated a major reassessment of policy which in turn was responsible for the political and economic changes which will be discussed later.

11. See Kariuki, *Mau Mau Detainee* (London: Oxford University Press, 1963), pp. 178, 179 for an example of the adoration and reverence for Kenyatta as "the greatest African of them all," rising above tribal or racial hatred.

12. Montagu Slater, *The Trial of Jomo Kenyatta*, (2nd rev. ed.; London: Secker and Warburg, 1957).

13. Kariuki, *op. cit.*, pp. 22, 23.

14. Rosberg and Nottingham, *op. cit.*, p. 278.

15. Kariuki, *op. cit.*, p. 182.

16. Kenya Colony and Protectorate, *A Plan to Intensify the Development of African Agriculture in Kenya* (Nairobi: Government Printer, 1954); hereafter referred to as the Swynnerton Plan.

17. Carl G. Rosberg, Jr., "Independent Kenya: Problems and Prospects," *Africa Report*, VIII (December, 1963), 3, 4. Several other writers have agreed that in retrospect the Emergency regulation restricting African political organizations to the local level only served to aggravate existing tensions between the racial and tribal groups. See Marion Elizabeth Doro, "Kenya: A Case Study of the Development of Western Political Institutions in a Plural Society" (Ph.D. dissertation, University of Pennsylvania, 1959).

18. Great Britain Colonial Office, Report of the Kenya Constitutional Conference, Cmd. 1960 (London: H.M.S.O., February, 1960).

19. For a summary of voting arrangements for the legislative and executive branches see Susan Wood, *Kenya: The Tensions of Progress*, 2nd ed. (London: Oxford University Press, 1962), pp. 69, 70. Miss Wood described the Lancaster House decision to establish an African majority in the legislature and the introduction of a common roll franchise as "the end of much woolly thinking in British policy and consequent lack of direction," pp. 77, 80.

20. *Ibid.*, pp. 90, 91. The smaller tribes' fears of domination by Kikuyu and Luo were acknowledged by the Kikuyu. See Kariuki, *op. cit.*, pp. 165, 166.

21. *Kenya Education Commission Report*, Part II (Nairobi: Government Printer, 1964), para. 225.

22. Rosberg, Jr., *op. cit.*, p. 5.

23. The Sessional Paper of 1957 gave details as to the high priority to be placed upon the implementation of the Swynnerton Plan and to the development of the African economy in general. Kenya Colony and Protectorate, *Sessional Paper no. 77 of 1956/57: The Development Programme 1957/60* (Nairobi: Government Printer), pp. 4, 5, 46-57.

24. Cohen, *op. cit.*, pp. 93-107.

25. *The Economic Development of Kenya: Report of a Mission Organized by the International Bank for Reconstruction and Development* (Baltimore: Johns Hopkins Press, 1963), pp. 4, 5, and Chapter IV; hereafter cited as World Bank Survey.

26. The Royal Commission of 1953-55 (Cmd. 9475) recommended in 1955 that land be made available on a nonracial basis (Chapter 25). This confirmed the report by Special Commissioner L. G. Troup that much more intensive use could be made of the highlands; Kenneth Ingham, *A*

History of East Africa, p. 344. In 1959 a Government white paper on land policy agreed to the principle of opening the highlands to Africans. For details of the implementation of the plan see Susan Wood, *op. cit.*, pp. 28-32.

27. The Land Scheme distinguished between yeoman (experienced) and peasant (inexperienced, small-lot) farmers, and required large amounts of external capital. For a detailed account of the scheme see Susan Wood, *op. cit.*, pp. 84-87 and World Bank Survey, Chapter IV.

28. Besides the World Bank Survey, the best analysis of the Kenyan economy during the late 1950's is Marion W. Forrester, *Kenya To-Day: Social Prerequisites for Economic Development* (Gravenhage: Mouton & Company, 1962).

29. Cambridge Conference, p. 14.

30. Nigeria Federal Ministry of Education, *Investment in Education, The Report of the Commission on Pre-School Certificate and Higher Education in Nigeria* (Lagos: Government Printer, 1960); hereafter referred to as the Ashby Report.

31. The report was based on manpower estimates provided by Professor Frederick Harbison of Princeton University, who remained the leading proponent of this approach in the 1960's. Harbison's book, co-authored with Charles A. Myers, *Education, Manpower and Economic Growth* (New York: McGraw Hill, 1964) became a major watershed in the field. For further treatment of the approach, see *Manpower Aspects of Educational Planning* (Paris: HEP, UNESCO, 1968).

CHAPTER V

Education for Independence: 1956-63

THE CHANGING EDUCATIONAL SCENE

Against a background of dramatic political and economic activity, Kenya's educational system underwent a series of changes. Alan Pifer's description of the educational transformation necessary to prepare Nigeria for Independence is equally relevant to the situation in Kenya:

A system of education which during most of its system of development was geared to the special requirements of a colonial territory will inevitably have to be refashioned if it is to be the instrument through which the new political, social and economic expectations of a free African state are to be met (1).

This chapter examines Kenya's educational system—particularly the demands of the African community and the impact of external public reports and policy statements in shaping education—during the critical period from the mid-1950's to the achievement of Independence in 1963 (2).

Throughout the 1950's, the Beecher Report remained the basis for the Government's policy on African education. During the Mau Mau Emergency and the period of political uncertainty which followed, there was no serious attempt to reformulate educational policy. L. J. Campbell, headmaster of the Alliance High School, Kikuyu, describing the situation in 1963, stated that "since Beecher the planning and policy has only been a hand-to-mouth affair (3)."

During the Emergency many of the independent schools were closed for their allegedly subversive role in the uprising; the Government later encouraged these schools to reopen as soon as possible under mission or District Education Board management (4). However, the Kikuyu Independent Schools Association (KISA) was divided in its reaction to Beecher's recommendations that the independent schools be treated as reputable voluntary agencies. While some Kikuyu in Nyori and Kiambu districts preferred the jurisdiction of the District Education Boards to indoctrination by either Mau Mau or the missions, the Provincial Committee of the KISA, led by Jomo Kenyatta, opposed the Beecher plan. Although a significant number of independent school teachers and students were involved in Mau Mau, a careful study of detainees indicated that they "did not provide a higher proportion of Mau Mau adherents than those under mission management (5)." When, after the short-term instability caused by turning loose 400 teachers and some 10,000 students, the schools reopened, the vast majority of local school committees chose the secular management of the District Education Board over the jurisdiction of the missions (6).

As the responsibility for education passed increasingly into African hands, there was a growing recognition that education's role in the territory was changing. In 1957 the Minister of Education, Labor and Lands, Mr. Coutts, expressed misgivings about multiracialism when he cited school integration difficulties in Little Rock, Arkansas as an example of trying "to force certain views on certain people (7)."

The Sessional Paper of 1956/57 stated that the purpose of the development program for 1957-60 was to maintain European standards, to raise Asian standards, and to create African standards, thus affirming the intention to redress racial imbalances. But this declaration was not translated into action, for the allocation of funds revealed that the European community, one percent of the population, would receive 19 percent of the budget, the Asian community, three percent of the population, would receive 28 percent, and the African community would receive only 53 percent of funds available for education (8). Despite these severe financial limitations, the clamor for greater educational opportunity for Africans became so intense that by 1960 the number of African primary schools was more than twice that forecast by Beecher, while there were three times as many intermediate and secondary schools as projected in the plan.

In 1961, during the period of responsible government, when Ronald Ngala, the leader of KADU, was Minister of Education, he found himself in the awkward position of having to explain the reasons for racial distinctions in education and defending the system as doing the best job possible (9). KANU spokesmen took strong exception to Ngala's praise of the situation and demanded a more equitable division of funds (10). For a variety of reasons, however, racial segregation of schools remained a persistent problem. In 1963, the General Secretary of the Kenya National Union of Teachers, S. J. Kioni, wrote that "no true integration has taken place, despite many statements by the Kenya Government (11)."

Sheldon Weeks has pointed out that both before and since Independence, the popular demand for education in Kenya far exceeded the Government's ability to provide enough schools (12). In sponsoring his famous "airlifts" of students to the United States before Independence, Tom Mboya capitalized on the popular demand for education by circumventing official channels. But qualitative changes were also a major concern, and in 1961, Mboya described a new movement to Africanize education:

We have had in this country an educational system geared to meet a colonial psychology and a colonial atmosphere. That kind of education has created a kind of educated person that, to a large extent, would fail to meet the new emotional, psychological and social problems that will arise after independence and nationhood. . . . Our new system must aim at eliminating . . . this colonial psychology and creating a truly independent psychology aimed at instilling in the minds of our boys and girls, the pride that they are Africans. It must begin to move to give a greater appreciation of African culture, African history and the African personality . . . (13).

At the same time, another member of Parliament described a new, less rote-oriented type of education which he felt was necessary to create constructive citizens in Kenya: civics, for example, should not merely require learning the names of political leaders, but, in order for democracy to succeed, should enable students to understand how the Government worked (14). After Independence, S. J. Kioni proposed that education for citizenship involve students in national schemes such as adult literacy drives. Kioni went on to urge that every administrative post be Africanized, that African history and literature be taught, and that the national anthem be sung in school every morning (15).

Not only the psychological and political aspects of education were undergoing a transformation during the early 1960's. For example, in 1961, Minister of Education Ngala stressed the role that educational expenditures would have on overall development (16); increasing attention was given to the problem of relating education to specific manpower priorities. Greatly stimulated by the Ashby Report in Nigeria, education was, in Guy Hunter's words, suddenly "becoming directional—part of a social policy for growing countries—and manpower surveys and commissions are the order of the day (17)."

In Kenya, the growing demand for secondary-level skilled manpower placed particularly heavy demands on the still-inadequate facilities. A report by the Laurence Commission on teachers' salaries noted that attempts to upgrade salaries would have to compete for funds with the expansion of secondary schools (18). Recognition of the scarcity of funds and qualified teaching personnel led to the recruitment of foreign teachers through such programs as the Anglo-American Teachers for East Africa (TEA) in 1961 and the Peace Corps in 1964. TEA was started as a result of a conference in Princeton, New Jersey, in December, 1960, under the auspices of the African Liaison Committee of the American Council on Education. The Princeton Conference, as it came to be known, stressed East Africa's need for large amounts of external aid before it would be able to direct its own development. Educational aid, the Conference asserted, should be concentrated at the critical bottleneck at the secondary level (19).

Although Africanization was achieved much more rapidly in the administrative sphere of education than in the classroom, the secondary school teachers supplied by TEA were enthusiastically welcomed by most African leaders. Dr. Kiano, Kenya's delegate to the Princeton Conference and later Minister of Education, stated that it "was one conference where we achieved results (20)." Soon after Independence, Mr. Otiende, then the Minister of Education, recognized the great contribution of and continuing need for expatriate teachers (21); this need was subsequently affirmed by the Kenya Government's use of several hundred expatriate teachers per year.

Besides the quantitative needs for funds and personnel, important qualitative changes, begun during the early 1960's, had considerable impact on Kenyan education. Research became a significant factor as studies on child development and curriculum were carried out at the Institute of Education at Makerere College in Uganda. With aid from the Ford Foundation, a "Special Center" was set up in Nairobi to study the use of language in schools (22); it later merged with other research units to become the Curriculum Development Research Center.

The fundamental problem of adapting education to realistic local needs remained as difficult as it had been at the time of the Phelps-Stokes Reports. Progress was made in changing curricular emphasis from British culture to African culture (23), but the British tradition of humanistic education survived in spite of the practical needs fostered by Kenya's predominantly rural subsistence society (24). The British tradition endured in Kenya largely because efforts to develop agricultural training programs often were still seen as offering a second-rate education, as they generally had done during the colonial era.

New developments in Kenya's educational system created new problems. With the expansion of primary schools outpacing that of secondary schools, hundreds of thousands of Kenyan children were left in what Margery Perham refers to as a "mental no-man's land (25)." Separated from their own village culture by new expectations, many primary school leavers were unable to find skilled jobs or further educational opportunities. The most apparent fruits of their academic labors were frustration and disappointment (26), and it became increasingly clear that the economic, social, and political consequences of the growing urban and rural unemployment were to be a critical problem for African leaders (27).

The Decline of the Missions

Throughout the period immediately preceding Independence, the role of voluntary agencies remained remarkably stable. In 1960, referring to the Beecher Report's insistence that education be based upon sound moral and spiritual foundations, Mr. Mathieson, then Minister of Education, stated that "the Government still completely adheres to this proposition as the fundamental basis for any satisfactory system of education, and we very much welcome and value the continued cooperation of the voluntary agencies in the development and management of our schools (28)." Soon after Independence, Mr. Otiende confirmed the importance of the voluntary agencies (29), but it quickly became evident that there would be a shift in church-state relations.

In the light of Government encroachment upon the management of church schools in Uganda and in several other newly independent nations, the Christian churches in Kenya issued a joint statement expressing their determination to continue their service in the educational field. Indicating hope that their "divine commission [would] . . . be safeguarded," the missions' representative wrote:

Bearing in mind our long accumulated experience in education in Kenya we want to be able to place at the service of the State the further service of our teaching staff and to have our members participate on education committees concerned with planning, policy and professional research (30).

Although the teachers' union welcomed the statement (31), Otiende soon made it clear that the missions no longer enjoyed a privileged position in the field of education in Kenya. Speaking at a conference sponsored by the Christian Council of Kenya at Limuru, Otiende acknowledged the great educational contributions that the churches had made and would continue to make, but stressed that the new demands of an independent Kenya would require a more unified approach to the educational enterprise (32) than had been created during the years of mission dominance.

Higher Education

Changes in higher education came about largely as a result of the report of the Lockwood Commission in 1958, which urged that the Royal Technical College in Nairobi be reorganized as a federated university college within an East African University (33). The name was soon changed to the Royal College, and faculties of arts, science, engineering, and professional studies were developed in cooperation with Makerere College in Uganda. In 1962 a third university college was established at Dar es Salaam, Tanganyika, and in June, 1963, the three colleges were officially united in the University of East Africa (34).

A conference held at the Rockefeller Foundation's villa on Lake Como in October, 1963, emphasized the University's determination to remain federated (35). Its Vice-Chancellor, Sir Bernard de Bunsen, in stressing such advantages of continued federation as economy—particularly avoiding duplication of services—and the maintenance of international standards, closely followed the recommendations of the UNESCO Conference on the Development of Higher Education in Africa held at Tananarive, Malagasy Republic, in

September, 1962 (36). In retrospect, it is clear that the Como conferees' pragmatic approach resulted from the realistic projection of available funds rather than from the rhetoric of the Tananarive Conference.

THE EVOLUTION OF EDUCATIONAL POLICY

Despite the limitations of long-range planning, there was a growing realization that a comprehensive survey of Kenya's educational needs was required to give direction to the country's economic and political development. Ronald Ngala had proposed in 1961 "a formal inquiry into our education policy with a view to formulating a plan for the next eight years which will be within the expected financial resources of the country (37)."

The reaction of other members of the Legislative Council was generally enthusiastic, and Dr. Kiano spoke for many when he hoped "that the Beecher Report is dead and that we will start a new phase in our educational system (38)." Mr. Gichuru called for less criticism of the Beecher Report and more support for positive action for the new survey (39). In referring to the proposed commission's terms of reference, Mr. Sagini suggested that it study the "whole problem of education," adding, "I think its composition should be like the proverbial bikini, large enough to cover the subject (40)." However, despite the widespread recognition that such a study was necessary, the proposed survey was not undertaken until after Independence, when the Ominde Commission was appointed to carry it out. Several major reports were published in the meantime, with varying degrees of relevance to the Kenya situation.

The Addis Ababa Report

The first of these was the Report of the Conference of African States on the Development of Education in Africa, which met at Addis Ababa in May, 1961, under the joint sponsorship of UNESCO and the United Nations Economic Commission for Africa. Although not yet independent, Kenya was among the 39 African states participating (41). The goal of the Addis Ababa Conference was "to provide a forum for African States to decide on their priority educational needs to promote economic and social development in Africa, and in the light of these, to establish first tentative short-term and long-term plans for educational development in the continent, embodying the priorities they had decided upon for economic growth of the region (42)."

The Conference's Report stressed Africa's need for more and better educational opportunities, and suggested as a general goal that the substance of education be adapted to fit the era of Independence (43). Although some mention was made of the need for agricultural training and community development, the Report emphasized more academic reform, such as the inclusion of African history and culture in the curriculum, and the importance of meeting the high-level manpower requirements of emerging nations (44). In determining priorities, the Conference assigned greatest urgency to secondary and post-secondary education, stating that this must be put "before the goal of universal primary education if for financial reasons the two are not yet compatible (45)." Primary and adult education were to be developed at the same time, with a goal of universal literacy by 1980, but at the time of the Conference, the African nations' greatest concern was an adequate supply of skilled manpower. Perhaps the most widely discussed aspects of the Addis Ababa Report were the short-term and long-term goals which estimated the future educational targets of the continent. Expressed as percentages of the appropriate age groups, the proposed enrollments were (46):

	1960-61	1965-66	1970-71	1980-81
Primary	40	51	71	100
Secondary	3	9	15	23
Higher	0.2	0.2	0.4	2

Although the Report repeatedly stated that education was an investment which would pay for itself in the long run (47), the estimates of what such expansion would cost pointed to a massive financial commitment. The Report estimated that in order to meet their needs, African nations would have to allocate an increasing percentage of their national income to education, and despite considerable growth in available resources, their total annual deficits would rise to a high of over $1,000,000,000 in about 1970 (48). Massive amounts of external aid would be required to supplement African efforts, and the conference called on UNESCO as well as "all States and countries and all non-governmental organizations which have taken part in the conference to support and share in the implementation of the present resolution (49)."

The Report frequently stated that the plan was only intended to serve as a guide to aid each territory in determining its own educational needs (50), and Karl Bigelow notes that despite the general acceptance of the short- and long-term plans, the notion of planning for educational development was more important than the actual plans (51). Furthermore, the influence of the Ashby Report upon the Addis Ababa Conference was reflected in the growing recognition "of education as an investment in any program of economic and social development, and the need for a close link between educational planning and over-all development planning (52)."

AFTER ADDIS

In accordance with resolutions of the United Nations General Assembly and the Economic Commission for Africa, the Ministries of Education of the African countries met in Paris at the UNESCO office ten months after Addis Ababa to discuss the implementation of the plan (53). The Ministers agreed that machinery for educational planning was necessary in each country, and recommended that UNESCO help by arranging study grants and seminars on educational planning (54). The Paris Conference reaffirmed the high priority given to teacher training and the entire range of secondary education, but high priority was also assigned to rural schools. The participants further resolved that special attention should be devoted to adult education because of the relatively cheaper and faster returns in increased productivity (55). Thus, even at the peak of the "high-level manpower" era, there was a recognition of education's role in upgrading the vast majority of the population who had had little or no formal schooling. In the country-by-country progress report, Kenya stood fairly well, having almost achieved universal primary education for four years, with ten percent of those completing four years gaining entrance to intermediate education facilities (56).

The next meeting on the implementation of the Addis Ababa Plan was held in Leopoldville (now Kinshasa) in February and March, 1963, under the auspices of the Economic Commission for Africa. The Leopoldville meeting reaffirmed the resolutions of the Paris Conference, but called for more aid from UNESCO and other sources to help African nations meet the budget deficits resulting from increasing educational expenditures. The meeting called for creation of a permanent conference of African Ministers of Education which would continuously review the implementation of the Addis Ababa Plan (57).

The Tananarive Report

The Conference on the Development of Higher Education in Africa was convened at Tananarive in September, 1962, under the auspices of UNESCO and the United Nations Economic Commission for Africa. Aside from limiting its discussion to higher education, the Tananarive Conference used generally the same approach as the Addis Ababa Conference in estimating the qualitative and quantitative educational changes necessary to meet the manpower requirements of developing nations. Three commissions—on problems in staffing, financing, and curriculum of higher education in Africa—were established (58).

The Tananarive Conference estimated the growth in enrollment which would be required by 1980 in order to ensure projected economic and social development. For Middle Africa (59), the higher-education enrollment target rose from .35 percent of the relevant age group in 1965 to 1.51 percent in 1980. Although the percentage. of students studying outside the African continent was expected to decline in relation to the total number of university students, the absolute number of students abroad was expected to rise until the end of the decade, thus requiring continued assistance from overseas institutions (60).

In keeping with the goals of supplying sufficient manpower, the Tananarive Report distinguished between degree and nondegree students, and recommended that the percentage of students enrolled in science and technology courses be increased to 60 percent, those in agriculture from four percent to eight percent (61). In order to get the best educational value for the investment of manpower and funds, the Report argued that the ratio of students to staff must rise considerably, and 5,000 students was agreed upon as the minimum size of a university institution in Africa (62). To avoid duplication and dissipation of scarce resources, the conferees concluded that the needs of Middle Africa could best be met by limiting the number of institutions of higher education in that region to 32 (63).

Like the figures given in the Addis Ababa Report, those given in the Tananarive Report were less important than the implications which they had for the formulation of policy. For example, the Tananarive Report acknowledged that the estimates would require periodic review, and stressed the necessity of developing machinery for collecting and compiling statistics and forming comprehensive plans within each territory (64). Throughout the Conference the need for cooperation among the African territories and aid from outside agencies was recognized as basic to the future development of the continent (65). The Tananarive Report stressed that in order to accomplish these tasks, African institutions of higher education could not become "ivory towers detached from the society in which they are situated," but must contribute to national unity within the states they serve (66). The Report acknowledged the difficulty of developing institutions which would be uniquely applicable to local needs without losing international status or academic freedom (67).

The Griffiths Report

Against the international background of the UNESCO Conference and the rapid emergence of many new nations in Africa, several reports referring specifically to education in Kenya were prepared in the years just prior to Independence. Without implying a direct causal relationship, it is clear that these reports reflected the approaches of the Addis Ababa and Tananarive Conferences.

In July, 1962, KANU requested V. L. Griffiths, a Cambridge professor with many years' experience in Africa, to prepare a background paper on education. Griffiths modestly described this brief paper, based on a three-week visit, as merely "suggestions (68)," but although the report was never referred to publicly, it apparently impressed policy makers, since Griffiths was called back to Kenya to serve as a consultant to the post-Independence Education Commission.

Recognizing the particular need to enable Kenya's 97 percent African population to assume a greater role in running the country, Griffiths identified the two main demands of the territory upon the educational system as trained African manpower and a sense of purpose and national unity (69). Before making specific suggestions on ways to meet these interrelated but frequently conflicting demands, Griffiths distinguished between two phases in future educational policy, while declining to restrict himself to arbitrary cutoff points such as those in the Addis Ababa five-year and two-year plans. Griffiths defined phase one as the period of urgency in which a new government, handicapped by a nearly empty exchequer, would have to establish itself in the eyes of its citizens and of the world at large; phase two would be reached when the economy had developed sufficiently to allow for maneuverability, and large-scale plans could be undertaken (70).

Griffiths was far more specific in pointing out the immediate task facing Kenya in the initial phase than in his consideration of long-term developments. In noting the pressing need for trained manpower, Griffiths gave the development of secondary-level education the highest priority, although he recognized that this "most urgent task" would have to be modified to some extent in order to satisfy popular aspirations, and that striking a balance between the conflicting interests was essentially a political rather than an educational problem (71).

In evaluating the advantages and disadvantages of Kenya's new African Government compared to its colonial predecessor, Griffiths stressed the idea that despite the population's general increased enthusiasm—which could be channeled into payment of school fees—the Kenyan Government, since it was naturally dependent on popular support to a far greater degree than the colonial regime had been, would have to devote more attention to public relations to maintain that popular support than the colonial administration had done. He conceded that the new Government would have little scope for experiment or flexibility during phase one (72).

He also noted that in order to develop a sense of national purpose, or "intelligent patriotism," "outstanding Africans" were essential participants in the educational system, to give both teaching and textbooks a "Kenyan flavor," although foreign teachers would be required for some time to come (73). This emphasis on the qualitative value of Africanization marked a significant departure from the Beecher and Binns Reports, and indicated the extent to which the concept of education for nation-building was bound to political considerations.

Before examining the growing economic demands upon education, Griffiths raised a fundamental question: should education be considered a social service or an investment? He indicated that although such a distinction was not absolute, the belief in the right of every individual to a primary education would have to be weighed against the importance of education as a vital aspect of national development (74). Griffiths stressed the importance of formulating a comprehensive plan for the most effective allocation of resources. While his suggestions did not constitute a manpower survey in the quantitative sense (75), they were intended to clarify certain qualitative issues which the new Government would have to face. In a brief review of the educational system Griffiths concluded that, with such notable exceptions as agricultural training, the existing facilities met the country's quantitative manpower needs in a time of recession (1962).

Griffiths felt that until the economy took a sufficient upward turn, no major expansion would be possible, and that the primary concern during phase one should be qualitative changes including the coordination of subprofessional training (intermediate-level manpower) and the raising of its status, and the coordination and extension of experimental and developmental projects (76).

In turning to less-skilled manpower, small farming in particular, Griffiths raised another fundamental question, namely what the schools could and could not do. Addressing himself to the persistent problem of agriculture, Griffiths asked: "What are we up against? Ignorance? Bad habits? An intensive desire to get away from the old rural life?" He concluded that new atittudes and habits were far more important than theoretical knowledge (77). He arranged a listing of what schools could teach, in order of increasing difficulty and expense:

Information and working under orders—the easiest and cheapest to teach because memory of facts could be tested by examination.

Practical crafts, science, etc.—relatively easy, but more expensive, because of need for equipment and smaller classes.

Judgment, imagination, and initiative—active qualities of the mind, more difficult because of their decreased dependence on examinations and greater dependence on the skills of the teacher. Since teachers of the necessary quality are rare, such requirements become considerably more expensive.

Changes in attitudes—extremely difficult to accomplish "and sometimes impossible" because of the number of factors involved outside the school.

Adult experience of working conditions—not possible to accomplish within the formal school situation (78).

Griffiths concluded that the most realistic approach to the problem of small farming in Kenya should combine practical demonstrations for adults, experimental agricultural training for the young, and highly developed propaganda for the entire community to stem the migratory rush to the urban areas (79).

Although Griffiths' approach to the subject was less precise than that of some other reports, his treatment of basic considerations was refreshingly direct. In retrospect, the greatest contribution of the Griffiths Report was not the formulation of policy, but the clarification of issues, particularly the recognition that a decision regarding the allocation of resources would be a political one for which Kenya's new leaders would bear the ultimate responsibility.

The World Bank Survey

At the request of the Governments of Kenya and Great Britain, the International Bank for Reconstruction and Development undertook a survey of the economic development of Kenya in 1961 (80). A ten-member mission spent three months in Kenya in late 1961, studying all aspects of Kenya's economic development, and education was treated as one among many sectors of the economy competing for funds. The education advisor on the mission was C. Arnold Anderson, Director of the Comparative Education Center at the University of Chicago, and most of his recommendations (81) were included—in abridged form—in the final report. Indicating the relatively low priority assigned to education, the Survey contained one chapter on "Social Services and Manpower," which included discussions of education, health, and housing; 17 of the 311 pages in the final publication were devoted to the section on education.

Agriculture was given top priority, based on the fact that over three-quarters of Kenya's population and annual income were involved in some form of agricultural activity. To the extent that a second priority was identified, the World Bank mission placed considerable emphasis on the development of human resources. Although there was substantial overlapping between items within the overall proposed programs, the allocation of funds gives an idea of the relative importance in the commission's view of the various sectors. Out of a total development program of £56,000,000 agricultural and related schemes such as irrigation projects were to receive over £8,500,000 while education was to receive £2,600,000. Another £2,300,000 was allocated to localization, or Africanization, and training (82), which the mission discussed under the heading of "Manpower."

Although the distinction may appear to be merely one of semantics, it draws attention to the failure of the World Bank Survey to deal with education as an investment in human resources. By leaving the question "Social service or investment?" unanswered, the Survey failed to integrate education and manpower development within a scheme for overall economic development. Since the mission dismissed the idea of a manpower survey as premature (83), it is not surprising that its numerous proposals for Kenya's development appear to be more the work of a committee of individuals working separately than a well-integrated plan (84).

In its consideration of education, the mission, like several of its predecessors, pointed to the bottleneck at the secondary level as the most critical education need, requiring large numbers of expatriate teachers as well as qualitative improvements in teacher training (85). Despite popular demands, the Survey did not recommend universal primary education at this point, and local school districts were urged to take the major financial responsibility for expansion at the primary level (86). Beyond these basic points, the World Bank Survey consisted primarily of a review of most of the persistent problems in Kenyan education: the small number of girls being educated, the difficulty in changing from the vernacular to Swahili or English, and the problem of improving agricultural production through improved agricultural training. The mission's recommendations were unimaginative at best (87). For example, as a "bold experiment" it suggested that double sessions be instituted at the primary level. This was not only inconsistent with the mission's stated policy of restraint, but was hardly a bold experiment, since overexpansion at the primary level had long been considered a problem (88).

When compared with other reports, the World Bank Survey suffered by trying to cover too much. The difficulty of condensing and weaving together the separate reports of the members of the mission was reflected in the watered-down tone of the final report. The compilation of statistics in the charts and tables made the Survey a useful reference source, but the failure to integrate studies of the various sectors of the developing economy into a cohesive plan provided a description of past accomplishments rather than a dynamic prescription for the future (89). It remained for Guy Hunter to provide Kenya with a detailed analysis of her educational needs during the critical years ahead.

The Hunter Report

As a result of a preliminary manpower-need assessment of East Africa conducted by Guy Hunter and Frederick Harbison in the summer of 1962 (90), the Institute of Race Relations and Political and Economic Planning (PEP) sponsored the expansion and publication of the study as *Education For A Developing Region* (91). Although Hunter's main concern lay with Kenya's critical need for skilled manpower, he acknowledged, like Griffiths, that the economic demands of the state would have to be balanced with the political demands of individuals, and possibly with a third factor, educational theory (92).

Hunter considered his task to be the compilation of a "detailed case study of the actual day-to-day problems of educational policy" in a particular area. He perceived the problems to exist on two levels. The first was the "staggering" increase in the number of primary school leavers, which was outpacing efforts to expand secondary education, and bringing strong pressure to bear for more rapid expansion. The danger in this situation was that quality would be sacrificed for quantity, with the eventual effect of lowering university standards, as had already occurred in other developing states, such as Burma (93). Hunter felt the second crisis occurred after secondary school, when the sharp increase in secondary school leavers would lead to violent pressure for expansion of the "sixth forms (94)." In both cases the basic need was to strike a proper balance not only between quality and quantity education, but between academic and practical curricula. Along with the problem of language, Hunter considered the humanistic tradition of education one of the colonial legacies which the new Government would have to modify (95). He concluded that East Africa would have to develop various types of institutions to provide manpower at intermediate levels (96); technical or vocational schools were to maintain standards of quality as high as those of academic institutions.

Hunter's report dealt with Tanganyika and Uganda as well as Kenya, but discussed the facilities and needs of the three territories separately. It noted Kenya's particular reliance upon the capital and skills of Europeans in agriculture and industry, and those of Asians in commerce, indicated in estimates of racial distribution in high- and intermediate-level manpower categories in 1961. The first category included professional men of graduate or equivalent level, senior administrators, and managers in industry and commerce. The second included technicians and subprofessionals, civil service workers at the executive grade, middle management, and teachers with secondary education (97).

From the existing stock, Hunter estimated the rate of wastage, or the number who would leave their jobs during the period under study. He readily acknowledged the limitations of the estimates, but stressed that they could, "provided they are kept up to date and refined, . . . serve as a model or base-line upon which adjustments can be built." He anticipated that as a result of Africanization, up to 80 percent of the Europeans would leave within five years of Independence, but that a lower proportion of Asians, and very few Africans, would do so. In estimating Kenya's annual economic growth, Hunter allowed for such uncertainties as shifts in world prices and quotas for major export crops. He forecast a growth rate of two or three percent per year for the first five years, and 4½ percent from 1966 to 1971 (98). To determine the growth of manpower requirements, Hunter calculated the differential rates at which the two categories would grow: roughly double the growth rate for national income for Category I, and treble for Category II (99). From these estimates the requirements for 1961-66 could be derived, adding the high and low growth rates to wastage. If, after the initial period of replacing expatriates and establishing a stable government, a 4½ percent annual growth rate could be maintained, the manpower requirements from 1966-71 would continue to increase rapidly (100).

In looking at the projected supply, Hunter reviewed the capacity of the educational system and concluded that Kenya would not be able to meet even the minimum requirements for economic growth until 1966, and that from 1966 to 1971 massive external aid would be necessary if a growth rate of 4½ percent per annum were to be achieved.

In arriving at the estimates of demand and supply it is significant that Hunter never referred to the percentage of the total population that was literate, or to the percentage of the relevant age group attending secondary school, as had so many other studies. Kenya, like most developing nations, has a dual economy with a large traditional sector based on subsistence agriculture, and a small modern sector composed mainly of the public services; Hunter's calculations concerning skilled manpower were based entirely on the modern sector. However, he recognized that both sectors had to be provided for, and that education for the rural society at large was essential to Kenya's overall development and stability (101). After examining the total output of the educational system, Hunter drew three major conclusions: a) that expansion of secondary schools was the key to the problem of high-level manpower; b) that for the next five years or more, secondary school graduates should be used to man vital services, after a three-year training program to diploma or equivalent level; c) that teaching staff, notably scientists, were the key contribution from outside East Africa (102).

Hunter cited three possible shortcuts to be taken by African leaders: a) substitution of experience for educational certificates in order to upgrade adults; b) acceptance of shorter and simpler training for those professional tasks, such as rural doctor, which could in fact be adequately, if not perfectly, performed at that level; c) provision for entrance into university courses, in North America and elsewhere, for boys and girls who did not come up to the academic standards of the Higher School Certificate (sixth form) (103). Hunter strongly recommended all three, but warned of the danger of sacrificing quality for the sake of relaxing some seemingly unnecessary requirements (104).

Although the problem was technically outside his frame of reference, Hunter noted that the huge number of primary school leavers for whom no education or employment was available dwarfed all other educational issues. In reviewing the importance of maintaining a wide range of institutions, Hunter went on to warn against sacrificing quality at the university level to satisfy a temporary manpower shortage (105). This echoed the suggestion made by Professor Harbison in his preliminary survey that each Government should set up a permanent system for the development of human resources.

Harbison urged that a board be established in each territory with representatives of labor, management, and the various ministries to keep track of
manpower goals within a closely integrated program of overall development,
so that educational output would not outpace employment opportunities at
any level (106).

A CRITICAL SUMMARY

L. J. Lewis summarized the effects of political and economic change in
Africa by stating:

The movement toward political independence in Africa is accompanied by
rapid expansion of primary education, relatively large expenditures on higher
education, slower expansion of secondary education, and as yet inadequate
improvement of training facilities for teachers. Politically, there is a general
recognition of the importance of education for economic and social
development and the acceptance of the need to plan for it. But nowhere has
the planning been sufficiently integrated with the rest of the economic and
social planning (107).

The relevance of Lewis' statement to developments in Kenya is apparent from
the previous discussion. Despite the differences in scope and methodology
among the five reports on education in Kenya, it is clear that they share a
common view of the role of education within a developing nation, and their
proposals for concentrating on the bottleneck at the secondary level, relating
education more closely to manpower needs, are generally similar. It is
difficult to determine the extent to which the recommendations in the
various reports led to implementation of the proposals, but the creation of
the Teachers for East Africa program, and subsequently the Peace Corps,
were clear responses to the demand for expansion at the secondary level.
Although political leaders in Kenya publicly accepted the goals identified in
several reports (108), it was more difficult to put such verbal commitments
into practice.

An examination of the allocation of expenditures during the period of
nation-building provides a rough indication of the extent to which the policy
reports were implemented. For example, the percentage of Government
expenditure allocated to education rose from 13.3 percent in 1957-58 to 16.9
percent in 1961-62 (109), thus reflecting the view that investment in
education is a means of accelerating economic growth. But Sheldon Weeks
has attributed the dramatic expansion of education during the late 1950's, to
more than twice the targets set by Beecher, more to African demands than to
governmental plans (110). During this same period, shifts within the
education budget showed similar changes, as the proportion allocated to the
African community rose from 57 percent to 61 percent. Of perhaps equal
importance, the percentage of funds being spent on secondary education rose
from 10.5 percent in 1955 to 14.2 percent in 1962 (111).

Although none of the documents of the 1950's was formally approved
and implemented to replace the Beecher Report, the acceptance in both word
and deed of the growing role of education in national development confirmed
the determination of the emerging nation to plan its own course. Whether
educational development in Kenya followed the recommendations of the
reports described, or whether the reports merely reflected the dramatic
changes on the social, political, and economic scene is immaterial. What was
significant at the eve of Independence was the recognition of the importance
of education to Kenya's future growth, and the allocation of responsibility
for shaping the educational system to the Africans themselves.

Notes

1. Alan J. Pifer, "Education: Bulwark of Nigerian Independence," *Africa in Transition* (The Kennecott Lecture Series, 1960-61, no. 6 [Tucson: The University of Arizona Press, 1961]), 26.

2. For a brief examination of the changing forces upon education throughout the continent see L. J. Lewis, "Education and Political Independence in Africa," *Comparative Education Review*, V, no. 1 (June, 1961), 39-49.

3. L. J. Campbell, headmaster of Alliance High School, Kikuyu, Kenya, letter to author dated December 16, 1963.

4. Kenya Colony and Protectorate, *Education Department Annual Report, 1953* (Nairobi: Government Printer), pp. 26, 27.

5. F. B. Welbourn, *East African Rebels*, pp. 160, 161.

6. Canon Bewes, "Missionary on Mau Mau," *Times Educational Supplement* (London), no. 1972, February 13, 1953, p. 134. Canon Bewes had been a CMS missionary in Kikuyu country from 1929-49.

7. Kenya Colony and Protectorate, *Legislative Council Reports*, November 5, 1957, pp. 437, 438.

8. Kenya Colony and Protectorate, *The Development Programme 1957/60: Sessional Paper No. 77 of 1956/57* (Nairobi: Government Printer, 1957), pp. 65-73.

9. Kenya Colony and Protectorate, *Legislative Council Reports*, LXXXVII (July 12, 1961), 2243, 2244.

10. *Ibid.*, July 19, 1961, p. 2536.

11. S. J. Kioni, "Kenya National Union of Teachers Newsletter," *Reporter*, III, no. 88 (1963), 26.

12. Sheldon Weeks, *Divergence in Educational Development: The Case of Kenya and Uganda* (New York: Teachers College Press, 1967) pp. 10, 11.

13. Kenya Colony and Protectorate, *Legislative Council Reports*, July 21, 1961, p. 2693.

14. *Ibid.*, July 19, 1961, p. 2557.

15. Kioni, "KNUT Newsletter," *op. cit.*, January 4, 1964, p. 15.

16. Kenya Colony and Protectorate, *Legislative Council Reports*, July 12, 1961, p. 2248.

17. Guy Hunter, *The New Societies of Tropical Africa* (London: Oxford University Press, 1962). p. 247. During the summer of 1962, Guy Hunter and Professor Harbison of Princeton University (the manpower consultant to the Ashby Commission) did a preliminary manpower survey of East Africa that formed the basis of Hunter's book, *Education for a Developing Region* (London: Allen and Unwin, 1963).

18. Kenya Colony and Protectorate, *Report of the Teachers' Salaries Commission* (Nairobi: Government Printer, 1961), pp. 1, 2.

19. American Council on Education, African Liaison Committee, *Report of Conference on Education in East Africa*, Princeton, New Jersey, December 2-5, 1960, pp. 2-9; hereafter referred to as the Princeton Conference.

20. Kenya Colony and Protectorate, *Legislative Council Reports*, July 19, 1961, p. 2541.

21. J. Otiende, "The Clamour for Learning," *East African Standard*, December 12, 1963, p. 12. In 1963, the Peace Corps took over the job of sending secondary teachers overseas and TEA became TEEA (Teacher Education in East Africa), shifting to the teacher training colleges. For more details on the administration of TEA and the program's relationship with the U.S. Agency for International Development and with the East African governments and institutions, see the "SemiAnnual Report from Teachers College, Columbia University to the Agency for International Development on the Teachers for East Africa Project," mimeographed.

22. For a more thorough review of educational research in the years before Independence, see P. G. Wingard's article in *Review of Educational Research*, XXXII, no. 2 (1962), 294, 297.

23. For example, African children studied African plants in botany and African geography and history gradually replaced European- and British-oriented subjects.

24. P. C. C. Evans describes the impractical, humanistic tradition in education which the Africans inherited from the British in "Western Education and Rural Productivity in Tropical Africa," *Africa*, XXXII, no. 4 (1962), 313-323.

25. Margery Perham, *The Colonial Reckoning* (New York: Knopf, 1962), p. 40.

26. Guy Hunter cited the isolation and frustration of primary school leavers and the gap between the education of boys and girls as two of the most serious current problems in African education in "Emerging Africans," *Adult Education*, XXII, no. 2 (Autumn, 1959), 101-107.

27. See Archibald Callaway, "Unemployment Among African School Leavers," *The Journal of Modern African Studies*, I, no. 3 (1963), 351-372.

28. Kenya Colony and Protectorate, *Legislative Council Reports*, LXXXV (May 17, 1960), 678, 679.

29. J. Otiende, "The Clamour for Learning," *op. cit.*, p. 12.

30. "Church Schools," *Reporter*, III, no. 94 (1963), 41. The statement was signed by Bishop Obadiah Kariuki of Fort Hall, the Chairman of the Christian Churches Educational Association and John J. McCarthy, the Catholic Archbishop of Nairobi.

31. S. J. Kioni, "Religion in the Schools," KNUT Newsletter, *op. cit.*, III, no. 95 (1963), 21.

32. While Otiende did not specify the nature of the changes, it soon became clear that the churches would be subject to more centralized control by the Government. "Church and State," *Reporter*, no. 100, February 14, 1964, 33. For an interesting analysis of changing church-state relations in African education see David G. Scanlon, *Church, State and Education in Africa* (New York: Teachers College Press, 1965).

33. East Africa, *Report of the Working Party on Higher Education in East Africa* (Nairobi: Government Printer, 1958). This report led to the publication of *Higher Education in East Africa* (Entebbe: Government Printer, 1958) by the Governments of Kenya, Tanganyika, and Uganda.

34. For an excellent survey of the interterritorial difficulties which have impeded progress towards an East African Federation, see Joseph S. Nye, Jr., "East African Economic Integration," *The Journal of Modern African Studies*, I, no. 4 (1963). A. J. Hughes stressed the political difficulties in *East Africa: The Search for Unity* (Baltimore: Penguin Books, 1963).

35. *Report of a Conference on the University of East Africa*, Villa Serbelloni, Bellagio, Italy, October 21-25, 1963, mimeographed; hereafter referred to as the Como Conference.

36. *Development of Higher Education in Africa* (Paris, UNESCO, 1963); hereafter referred to as the Tananarive Conference.

37. Kenya Colony and Protectorate, *Legislative Council Reports*, July 12, 1961, p. 2243.

38. *Ibid.*, July 19, 1961, pp. 2536, 2537.

39. *Ibid.*, July 21, 1961, pp. 2676, 2677.

40. *Ibid.*, July 21, 1961, pp. 2678, 2679.

41. Representing Kenya were W. D. Gregg, Permanent Secretary to the Ministry of Education and Director of Education, L. D. A. Baron, Deputy Secretary to the Treasury, D. T. A. Moi, Parliamentary Secretary of the Ministry of Education (and later Vice President), and W. Kimemia, Education Officer and Member of the Council of State. Addis Ababa Report, Annex II, p. 10.

42. Addis Ababa Report, p. v.

43. *Ibid.*, p. 3.

44. *Ibid.*, pp. 3-7.

45. *Ibid.*, p. 10.

46. *Ibid.*, p. 19.

47. *Ibid.*, pp. 11, 12. The influence of economics upon the Conference was apparent in the vast majority of background papers included in Annex IV. For example, Frederick Harbison (the manpower consultant for the Ashby Report and Guy Hunter's preliminary manpower survey) presented a paper on "The Process of Educational Planning," pp. 47-54.

48. The percentage of national income to be allocated for education would rise from 3.9 percent in 1961 to 8.6 percent in 1970, then level off at around 7 percent. *Ibid.*, p. 29.

49. *Ibid.*, p. 17.

50. *Ibid.*, pp. 29, 35.

51. Karl Bigelow, "Some Major Educational Problems in Africa South of the Sahara: A Critical Summary," *Journal of Negro Education*, XXX, no. 3, 346. Bigelow's article is an excellent summary of the Addis Ababa Report.

52. Addis Ababa Report, p. vi.

53. UNESCO, *Meeting of Ministers of Education of African Countries Participating in the Implementation of the Addis Ababa Plan* (Paris: UNESCO, March 26-30, 1962); hereafter referred to as the Paris Conference. Hon. A. Moi (Minister of Education) represented Kenya at the Conference.

54. *Ibid.*, p. 15.

55. *Ibid.*, p. 26.

56. *Ibid.*, p. 9.

57. United Nations Economic and Social Council, *Educational Development in Africa: Implementation of the Addis Ababa Plan*, Economic Commission for Africa (Leopoldville: February-March 1963), pp. 1-3.

58. *Ibid.*, p. 7. For more detail on the procedures and terminology see pp. 5-7 and 309-317 of the Tananarive Report.

59. For convenience, the report separated North Africa from the rest of the continent. Middle Africa refers to the sub-Saharan Africa north of the Republic of South Africa and the Portuguese territories.

60. Tananarive Report, pp. 2, 23. For an excellent analysis of the quantitative estimates of the Tananarive Report, see Karl Bigelow, "Implications of the Report of the Conference on the Development of Higher Education in Africa: For the Provision for Africans of Study Opportunities Overseas" (Teachers College, Columbia University, 1962), mimeographed.

61. Tananarive Report, pp. 23-25.

62. Present and projected student-to-staff ratios are given by various subjects, *Ibid.*, pp. 25, 26. Although the ratio would vary among subjects and institutions, the optimum average would rise from the present 7:1 to 15:1.

63. *Ibid.*, p. 37. For a complete list of the institutions see pp. 45, 46.

64. *Ibid.*, pp. 27, 28.

65. Mr. Adiseshiah, the Acting Director General of UNESCO, identified the call for cooperation as one of the most significant results of the Conference. *Ibid.*, p. 339.

66. *Ibid.*, p. 12.

67. *Ibid.*, p. 11, 12.

68. Griffiths stressed that he was merely making suggestions, not recommendations, and noted that in his three-week visit he had not dealt with such areas as university education, overseas scholarships, teacher training, and specific problems concerning the education of girls and the minority races in Kenya. Griffiths, "Some Suggestions for an African Government's Educational Policy in Kenya" (Oxford, 1962), typewritten; hereafter referred to as the Griffiths Report.

69. *Ibid.*, p. ii.

70. *Ibid.*, p. 1.

71. *Ibid.*, p. 1.

72. *Ibid.*, p. 4.

73. *Ibid.*, pp. 26, 27. For a more detailed discussion of the political role of education, see also pp. 24, 25.

74. Griffiths acknowledged the contribution of the Ashby and Addis Ababa Reports in promoting the notion of education for investment, pp. 7-9. In contrast, the Binns Report reflected the traditional concept of education as a social service, Binns Report, p. 131.

75. Griffiths referred to the preliminary manpower survey which Guy Hunter was undertaking with the aid of Professor Harbison. *Ibid.*, pp. 3, 18.

76. *Ibid.*, pp. 2, 18-20.

77. *Ibid.*, p. 13.

78. *Ibid.*, pp. 14-16. Griffiths elaborated further on these issues in his stimulating paper in the Kericho Conference volume. See Sheffield (ed.), *Education, Employment and Rural Development* (Nairobi: East African Publishing House, 1967).

79. Griffiths noted the American-sponsored secondary school at Chavakali as an example of hopeful experiments in this direction.

80. Although the World Bank mission's trip preceded Griffiths', their report was not published until 1963, so it is discussed here chronologically.

81. C. Arnold Anderson, "Education in Kenya, 1961-67," unpublished report prepared for World Bank Survey.

82. World Bank Survey, p. 62.

83. *Ibid.*, p. 211.

84. J. S. Skinner severely criticizes the Survey's lack of unity and focus in a book review in the *Journal of Modern African Studies*, I, no. 4 (1963), 551,552.

85. World Bank Survey, p. 309.

86. *Ibid.*, p. 227. The Survey acknowledged the widespread acceptance of the notion of universal education for seven years.

87. See *Ibid.*, p. 309 for a summary of the recommendations for education.

88. *Ibid.*, p. 227.

89. See the critical review by J. S. Skinner, *op. cit.*

90. Guy Hunter, "High-Level Manpower in East Africa: Preliminary Assessment." 2nd draft (consultant F. H. Harbison), unpublished, 1962. The publication *Education for a Developing Region* resulted from the initial survey; hereafter, Hunter Report refers to that publication.

91. Hunter Report, p. v.

92. *Ibid.*, p. 57.

93. *Ibid.*, pp. x, xi.

94. *Ibid.*, p. xi. Secondary schools in Kenya generally followed the British pattern of four "forms" followed by a qualifying examination which selects those for two additional years of "sixth form" work as preparation for the university.

95. The British tradition, largely transplanted in Kenya, was more concerned with the acquisition of the basic values of Western culture (i.e., religion, literature, history, etc.) than with learning practical skills. *Ibid.*, pp. 4-8.

96. Hunter Report, p. 58.

97. For a breakdown of these categories by main occupations, see Guy Hunter, "High Level Manpower in East Africa: Preliminary Assessment," 2nd draft, p. 7.

98. Hunter Report, pp. 58-9.

99. *Ibid.*, p. 59.

100. *Ibid.*, p. 60.

101. See also Hunter's later study, *The Best of Both Worlds? A Challenge on Development Policies in Africa* (London: Oxford University Press, 1967).

102. Hunter Report, p. 69. Hunter noted that the Anglo-American Teachers for East Africa scheme was attempting to remedy the need for teachers.

103. *Ibid.*, p. 106.

104. While granting that the insistence on paper qualifications might be less relevant in Kenya than in industrialized countries, Hunter stressed the importance of distinguishing between those skills for which the highest training is essential, and those in which something simpler will suffice. *Ibid.*, pp. 106, 107.

105. *Ibid.*, pp. 107, 108, 113.

106. For a detailed account of Harbison's suggestion, see Guy Hunter, "High Level Manpower," *op. cit.*, pp. 29, 30.

107. L. J. Lewis, "Education and Political Independence in Africa," *Comparative Education Review*, V, no. 1 (1961), 49.

108. J. Otiende, the Minister of Education, affirmed the Government's general commitment to the notion that investment in education would pay for itself in long-term economic and social development. "The Clamour for Learning," *op. cit.*, p. 12. James Gichuru, Minister of Finance, affirmed the quantitative targets of the Addis Ababa plan by stating that Kenya was trying to reach them. "Making Kenya a Good Bet for the Investor," *East African Standard*, December 12, 1963, p. 8.

109. World Bank Survey, p. 356.

110. Weeks, *op. cit.*, p. 10.

111. Taken from Kenya, *Education Department Annual Report, 1955*, pp. 37-40 and Ministry of Education, *Annual Report, 1962* (Nairobi: Government Printer), p. 41.

CHAPTER VI

Education for Nation-Building: 1964-70

During the 1960's, the orientation of education in Kenya shifted towards two urgent new priorities: training Africans to fill high-level positions, and the creation of a sense of national unity. Efforts by the Colonial Government to expand educational opportunity in the years immediately preceding Independence had coincided with an enormous and unparalleled public demand for education, and in the 1963 election campaign, the promise of universal free primary education was one of the basic planks in the KANU platform (1). Financial constraints have made the fulfillment of this promise a long-term goal at best, and it has remained a sensitive issue, at times an embarrassment to the Government.

The 1960's saw a dramatic resurgence of independent schools at the secondary level, as parents showed their determination to provide educational facilities beyond those which the Government could support. Although the establishment of any school without the approval of the Ministry of Education was officially illegal, politicians were among the worst offenders in opening self-help schools, and Government control was practically impossible. Adopting the Kiswahili phrase *Harambee,* meaning "Let's all pull together," from the KANU slogan, *Harambee* or self-help schools became a vital addition to Kenya's secondary school system.

In the area of higher education, the scarcity of opportunity within Kenya led many promising students to look beyond their country's borders. Thousands went overseas in the years preceding Independence, many without the official knowledge of the Government. Once again, politicians responded promptly to the demand. Tom Mboya, for example, organized several large airlifts of students to the United States. Although exact figures are unavailable, Kenya at the time of Independence probably had more students overseas in proportion to her total population than any other African country.

THE OMINDE COMMISSION

Against the background of growing demands on the educational system, the Minister of Education appointed a prestigious commission, headed by

Dr. Simeon Ominde, to review all aspects of education in Kenya (2). The Ominde Commission's report was less significant for the originality of its recommendations than for the expanded role in national development which it assigned to education. The Report marked a watershed in Kenya's educational history by setting a new tone appropriate to an independent African nation. While its consultants included such experts as V. L. Griffiths and Arthur Lewis, the members of the Commission were almost all Kenyan citizens, most of them experienced educationists.

It was the Commission's intention to lay down guidelines for the new nation, and to initiate "a beginning of continuous planning in Kenya (3)." The terms of reference, indicating the wide role which the new Government had determined to give educational planning, were:
1) appropriately to express the aspirations and cultural values of an independent African country;
2) to take account of the need for trained manpower to facilitate economic development;
3) to take advantage of the initiative and service of regional and local authorities and voluntary bodies;
4) to contribute to the unity of Kenya;
5) to respect the educational needs and capacities of children;
6) to have due regard for the resources, both in money and personnel, likely to become available for educational service; and
7) to provide for the principal educational requirements of adults (4).
Of these terms, the most significant were those stressing the role of education in two aspects of nation-building, promoting national unity through emphasis on cultural and social values and integrating education with overall economic planning.

The Report was published in two parts. The first part, completed at the end of 1964, dealt with questions of policy. The second section, providing mainly quantitative recommendations and a plan of priorities, was not made available until six months later, following the completion of the country's first major manpower survey. In setting out policy before clarifying priorities, the Report was unusual. The political and social role of education in the new society was a major theme in the first section; it asserted that the "educational system must help to foster a psychological basis of nationhood (5)." The Report suggested that this might be encouraged by greater integration of racially separate schools. The new Government had already officially prohibited segregation in schools, but putting this prohibition into effect was a slow task. The Commission was anxious to maintain the high standards of the former European schools, while opening them to children of other races. In the belief "that the secret of a national feeling which over-rides tribal and local loyalties lies in bringing about much more conscious mixing within our educational system (6)," it was suggested that each secondary boarding school should allocate at least 20 percent of its places to students from outside its region.

The Commission was also anxious that Kenyan schools should do more to promote and reinforce the nation's "own historic instincts and moral values." While recognizing that modernization would necessitate many social changes, the Report noted the importance of softening the impact of these changes by reducing the edge of competition typical in a western educational system and reemphasizing the "cooperative elements" in traditional African culture (7). Therefore, considerable attention was given to curriculum reform as a means of promoting greater knowledge and appreciation of Kenya's history and culture in the context of the other new nations, and teachers were expected to be "convinced exponents" of national unity. While the Report recommended that English be the universal medium of instruction in all schools, learning Kiswahili was to be compulsory in primary school "as a unifying national influence and a means of Pan-African communication over a considerable part of the continent (8)."

The Ominde Commission also had a mandate to consider the relationship between education and economic development. In the second part of its Report, the Commission took note of economic constraints effecting its recommendations for educational priorities. Kenya's first manpower survey had recommended a rapid expansion of higher and secondary education to meet serious personnel shortages at high skill levels. However, despite the lack of trained Africans for many high-level positions, the survey expressed concern over the capacity of the wage sector generally to absorb the large number of job-seekers. It added that "the most optimistic estimate of the total new non-agricultural employment that can be brought into being under the current 1966-1970 Development Plan will run around 15,000 jobs per year. . . . One of the heaviest responsibilities facing Kenya's educators is to devise ways and means of reorienting the aspirations and interests of most of the young people passing through the primary schools (9)."

The Ominde Commission took note of these economic priorities and, although it endorsed the ultimate goal of universal primary education, was at pains to demonstrate that this was not financially feasible in the immediate future. The Report calculated that on the most optimistic cost basis, Kenya could not achieve more than 80 percent enrollment of the eligible population in primary school by 1980. The Government was urged to concentrate on achieving a more equitable distribution of educational opportunities and on improving the quality of primary education. This reflected a desire to strengthen the content of instruction, but the Report also stressed that "nothing is more important than putting new heart into our primary teachers (10)." Recognizing that for some time to come, most primary teachers would not have received a full secondary education, the Report recommended the consolidation of teacher training colleges and the establishment of in-service training to upgrade teachers. The document also revealed a concern with diminishing employment opportunities for primary school leavers and with the orientation of primary education toward competition for places in secondary schools. It is therefore somewhat surprising that it opposed the introduction of vocational training in primary schools, and indicated little interest in reorienting the "aspirations and interests" of primary school leavers toward rural self-employment, or the extension of adult education to meet their needs.

While it accepted the importance of expanding secondary education, following the recommendations of the manpower survey, the Commission cautioned against an overprovision of secondary school places. By 1965 the rapid expansion of primary schooling had already led to a decline in the proportion of leavers able to enter Government-assisted secondary schools, and to a consequent increase in the number of *Harambee* schools (11). The Government plan, based on the manpower survey, allowed for expansion of the total enrollment of students in the first four years of government-sponsored secondary schools to 56,000 by 1970, and an even greater percentage increase in the small number of fifth- and sixth-year students, but this made no allowance for unassisted schools (12). The Ominde Commission sympathized in theory with the surge of local initiative which led to the rise of *Harambee* schools, and said, "Psychologically, the source of inspiration of the *Harambee* school is identical with underlying motives of the government's own development program (13)." Yet the Report warned that the growth of *Harambee* schools was not only "likely to produce strong local and tribal feeling, which are disruptive of a sense of nationhood," but was also in conflict with the national development plan, and would lead to unemployment and disappointment for many, increasing the threat of "resentment and unrest (14)." The Commission strongly urged the Government to arrest and control any further expansion of *Harambee* schools.

With the Report of the Ominde Commission, Kenya broke new ground in its educational history (15). The Report evidenced a belief in the school both as a vital instrument of economic development and as a central agent of social change. It emphasized that education in the future would reflect national rather than sectarian interests, and, above all, clearly showed that future educational decisions would inevitably reflect political as well as economic aims and constraints.

EXPANSION AND INTEGRATION

Since 1964 a remarkable expansion at all levels has taken place in Kenya. The rapid growth of primary school facilities in the late 1950's led to an even more dramatic expansion of secondary education in the 1960's.

Kenya, with 20 percent more people than Uganda, had, by 1965, "twice as many pupils attending schools, continuing in senior secondary schools and passing the school certificate," as Uganda (16). This educational boom has placed a particularly heavy burden on Kenya's resources. Between 1966 and 1968, educational expenditures increased by 40 percent, and by 1969, Kenya had one of the highest rates of such expenditure in all Africa, representing seven percent of the Gross Domestic Product (17). Although much of the necessary capital has come from overseas, Kenya now has a crushing burden of recurrent expenditures, and other areas of the economy have suffered accordingly. Moreover, expansion has been along essentially traditional lines; the more comprehensive integration of economic, manpower, and social planning attempted in Tanzania has not been implemented in Kenya (18).

Education for nation-building has become inseparable from political considerations. In quantitative terms, Kenya has maintained a comparatively good record in primary education. Reviewing the recommendations of the Addis Ababa Report, a UNESCO Conference in 1968 noted that primary enrollment in Africa had fallen short of the targets and that there was an average wastage of 32 percent between the first and sixth years (19). Kenya's record of primary expansion was better than the average, however, and in its seven-year system of primary education, wastage was only 21 percent (20).

Both the Government of Kenya and its citizens continue to look upon education as a productive investment. The 1970-74 Development Plan, for example, assigned "high priority" to universal primary education (21). Despite its already heavy educational expenditure, the Government proposed to increase enrollment from an estimated 61 percent in 1968 to 75 percent in 1974. The Plan stated that "a major instrument by which this enrollment target will be achieved is the remission of school fees." It is not clear whether the Government fully allowed for a population growth rate of approximately three percent, but the projected increase will involve an additional 600,000 primary school students by the end of the six-year period (22).

The expansion of primary education will of course be heavily dependent on the expansion of teacher training if standards are to be improved or even maintained. The 1966-70 Development Plan pointed out the need to reverse the trend toward untrained teachers by consolidating small teacher training colleges into larger and better equipped facilities (23). This goal was achieved, and by 1971, the proportion of unqualified primary school teachers had dropped from 31 percent to 24 percent. The second Plan established an ambitious program to reduce this figure to three percent by 1974, while increasing the supply of trained teachers from 27,400 in 1968 to 44,500 by 1974 (24).

The introduction of in-service training has contributed to the reduction in the number of untrained teachers, while the decrease in employment opportunities outside the school system has reduced wastage. In 1967, all teachers were awarded significant salary increases. The 1968 Education Act entrusted the management of primary schools to local authorities, but mounting demands from the Kenya National Union of Teachers led to the establishment of the Teachers Service Commission, empowered to "employ registered teachers (both primary and secondary), to assign teachers to any public school, to promote or transfer any such teacher, to terminate the employment of any such teacher (25)." Although salaries are still paid by local authorities and many teachers resist placement in any but their home area, the Teachers Service Commission has provided its members with greater financial security by guaranteeing these salaries, and has generally given the teaching profession a more secure status.

Salary increases and expanded training facilities, designed to upgrade the teaching profession, involve the Government in greatly increased expenditure; a high rate of population growth and current plans for the rapid expansion of primary education make it doubtful that educational quality can be maintained at present levels, much less improved. The 1970-74 Plan points out that cost projections are based on an increase from an average of 32 to 40 pupils per class (26). The Government's 1970 decision to introduce Kiswahili as the national language and medium of instruction in primary schools may further affect teacher quality and supply, as not all teachers are fluent in the language. Yet, despite financial constraints, the Government cannot afford to ignore the people's demands for education as a universal right.

Despite the increasing unemployment of school leavers at all levels, popular demand for secondary education remains strong. There is a danger that the experience of Eastern Nigeria may be repeated. There, the introduction of universal free primary education in the early 1960's led to enormous wastage and a rapid disillusionment with education as a worthwhile investment. A 1964 report on education in Eastern Nigeria concluded that "we are in great danger of facing a possible era of swing-back from universal popularity of and a belief in education to a scepticism as to its value and doubt as to whether it justifies the value set on it and the sacrifices it entails (27)." In fact, the 1970-74 Kenya Development Plan expresses the hope that the demand for *Harambee* schools will soon die a natural death because of the expenses involved to local communities and because "employment opportunities for the average school leaver have declined sharply (28)." However, as of 1971, the number of *Harambee* secondary schools was increasing rapidly; there were 478 unaided schools, out of a total of 809 schools, representing an enrollment of 59,676, out of a secondary school total of 140,719 (29). The growth of *Harambee* schools has been greatest in those areas with the largest percentage of primary school enrollment. Estimates suggest that over 50 percent of the 13- to 16-year old age group may be receiving some kind of schooling, including "repeaters" in the final year of primary school, in certain areas (30). Secondary enrollment has now far exceeded the estimates of manpower requirements put forward in the 1965 survey, and in the Government's development plans. Moreover, there has been some justification for the fears "that many of the children in these [*Harambee*] schools would not in fact receive an education that could justify the description of secondary (31)."

As late as 1965, the Government still officially deplored the expansion of secondary-school education outside the limits of its Development Plan (32). But because Kenya's leaders could not afford to ignore the political implications of local demands, many members of the National Assembly were directly involved in sponsoring *Harambee* schools. In 1966, a revised Development Plan for 1966-70 included provisions to extend aid to a limited number of *Harambee* schools (33). This revision was part of a plan to double the number of students in aided secondary schools by 1970. At the same time, Government inspection of *Harambee* schools was instituted and a new examination, the Kenya Junior Secondary Examination (KJSE), was introduced, to give *Harambee* students a certificate after two years of secondary education, since few *Harambee* schools offer more than two-year programs, and allow the transfer of some of the more able students to Government schools. In the short run, this has helped defuse unemployment as a political problem, but ultimately the Government will have to face the difficult task of integrating political demands for expanded educational opportunities with economic necessity.

Since Independence, Kenyan schools have acted to some extent as an integrative force. Racial integration in the former European and Asian schools advanced considerably in the mid-1960's and by 1967, Africans accounted for half the intake of all such schools (34). However, the former European schools, in particular, have maintained a high standard, necessitating a levy of fees far beyond the means of most African families. Since 1968, it has been Government policy to allocate half the first-year places in these schools to Africans, but the Ministry of Education has had to provide a large number of bursaries (full scholarships) in order to achieve even this balance. Although a large measure of integration has been achieved, the Government must choose between a desire to maintain the high standards of these schools and a desire to desegregate as rapidly and completely as possible. KJSE, for example, did much to integrate the secondary-school system. But the Ominde Commission's suggestion that 20 percent of secondary boarding students be drawn from regions other than that in which the school is located has not been carried out. In most secondary schools, a single ethnic group predominates, except at the fifth- and sixth-year levels. Although the tremendous expansion of secondary schools has undoubtedly made the attainment of secondary education less a social distinction than it had been, the whole educational system remains highly competitive. This is in contrast with the philosophy of the Tanzanian government, enunciated in the policy document, "Education for Self-Reliance," of integrating schools with the community on a socialist basis.

The contrasting emphases of Kenya and Tanzania on the role of education in fostering national integration may perhaps be seen most clearly at the university level. Tanzania has made strenuous efforts to create an educated elite committed to the goals of the nation and the betterment of the community. The political climate has activated an intellectual response in the University of Dar-es-Salaam and has encouraged a new historiography, which "attempts to build a model of the historical evolution of African nationalism which stresses the continuities more than the cleavages of that development (35)." It has also required direct governmental intervention in the affairs of the University, particularly in 1966, when large numbers of students were dismissed for opposition to a Government proposal that university graduates should spend a compulsory period in public service.

The desire to recoup part of the investment in university students in this way is easily understandable when the costs involved are considered. In addition to financing the education of many of its students abroad, Kenya increased the enrollment at the University of Nairobi by nearly 50 percent between 1968 and 1970, although the total annual cost of educating one student is roughly 30 times Kenya's per capita income. The 1966-1970 Development Plan stated that "it will continue to be Government policy to move increasingly towards loans as a method of financing the studies of students in post-secondary school education (36)." The implementation of this policy has proceeded slowly and bursaries still constitute the main source of government support. One advantage of the latter is that they enable the Government to guide students into priority manpower needs. Recipients of loans and bursaries are "bonded" to enter public service and stay for a minimum of three years. Nevertheless, Kenya has been more reluctant to interfere with the academic freedom of its university than has Tanzania.

The inauguration of the University of East Africa in 1963 represented a unique experiment in interterritorial integration. Not only did it minimize wasteful duplication, but it provided many opportunities for students from the different East African nations to study together and to develop an understanding of each other's problems and ideologies. The breakup of the University in 1970 into its constituent parts resulted from the desire of each country for a national university, symbolizing a growing national pride and divergence of national philosophies. While the new universities may contribute to nation-building along different lines in the former territories, the University of East Africa was potentially a factor for integration on a much broader basis.

CONTENT AND QUALITY

Combined with its expansion program, the Kenya Government has made strenuous efforts to improve the quality of the education provided. However, reform has largely taken place within an educational system patterned on that of Britain, rather than through a radical change in educational philosophy. The formal school system is highly competitive and has retained its strong academic orientation.

A major Government concern has been the lack of African teachers in the secondary schools. In 1966, there were only three Kenyan graduates teaching science in the secondary schools (37), but since then important steps have been taken to rectify this position. The University of Nairobi has a Department of Education which offers a bachelor's degree in education and a one-year post-graduate "diploma" course. Other trained secondary teachers are produced by Kenyatta College and the Kenya Science Teachers College, and there has been a marked improvement in the qualifications of candidates entering the training colleges. Between 1966 and 1970 the number of students enrolled in the three-year course for non-graduate secondary school teachers increased from 397 to 1,112 (38). As a result of these efforts, the Government has been able not only to appoint Kenyan citizens as headmasters in most secondary schools, but also to begin reducing the large number of expatriate teachers—70 percent of the staff in aided secondary schools in 1967—required to staff the schools.

The Government has also taken steps to coordinate all teacher training and link it with curriculum research. The Kenya Institute of Education (KIE), established in 1964, is the major instrument of this responsibility; in 1967, the Curriculum Development and Research Center (CDRC) became a part of the KIE. The KIE administers a scheme of examinations on behalf of the Ministry of Education, promotes in-service courses, provides advisory services to the Government, and is responsible for educational research (39). Much of the credit for the rapid development of both primary and secondary school curricula is due the Curriculum Development and Research Center. Its science section produces materials for both levels, and the mathematics section has produced textbooks for the East African School Mathematics Project, often called Entebbe Maths after the workshop held at Entebbe in 1963 to develop the "new mathematics," which is radically changing the teaching of math in East African schools. In addition to its research and production of materials for schools, the CDRC presents both radio and television programs over the Voice of Kenya, and sponsors workshops and in-service training courses for teachers in conjunction with the KIE (40).

The CDRC also developed the New Primary Approach (NPA), one of the most successful features of primary education in Kenya. This program was first developed to introduce Asian first graders to English as a classroom language in the late 1950's, but by 1966 half the first-grade classes in Kenyan primary schools were using it (41). However in 1970, when the Government decided to introduce Kiswahili as a national language, it was noted that "the practical . . . issues arising from the introduction of Swahili as the medium of instruction at the primary level are formidable (42)." The New Primary Approach, with its emphasis on learning rather than teaching, is both a way of improving the training of primary school leavers who staff primary schools, and a shift from passive rote-learning to an active, child-centered learning environment. Despite higher costs in the NPA due to the addition of more expatriate teacher training tutors and the creation of smaller classes, a determined effort has been made to improve supervision and increase the effectiveness of the approach, the training, and the materials involved.

In 1967, a unified syllabus was introduced for all Kenyan primary schools, noting that the function of a primary school was to give "a fundamental education in respect of literary, numerary, manual dexterity and general knowledge of the world (43)." It was hoped that emphasizing general education would serve both the small minority who did go on to further education, and the vast majority who did not go beyond primary school. Despite the attempt to introduce progressive pedagogy into the primary schools, many observers still regard the system as a straitjacket, because it continues to be based on a final examination. Until a better alternative becomes available, however, competitive national examinations will be inevitable. In an attempt to get away from the "failure" syndrome implicit in the use of the Kenya Primary Examination (KPE) as a filter between primary and secondary education, the KPE was replaced by the Certificate of Primary Education in 1967. Thus, all who complete the seven-year primary course receive recognition for their achievement. Many of the constraints inherent in Kenya's inherited educational system remain, and the New Primary Approach is still more an ideal than a reality, but it is designed to develop such vital nation-building qualities as curiosity and initiative, cooperation and toleration, and its very existence and preliminary implementation are hopeful signs for the future of primary education in Kenya.

The quality of secondary education in Kenya is much less homogeneous than that of primary education, the contrast lying mainly between aided and unaided schools. Most of the latter are *Harambee* schools, which are of a very poor standard in almost all respects. A report in 1966 showed that most had minimal and often unreliable financial support, poorly educated and trained staff, and very overcrowded classrooms. Thirty-five out of 47 *Harambee* headmasters surveyed had had no secondary education. Eight of their schools had laboratories, ten had libraries, and only half their students had even essential texts (44). In 1967, only 35 percent of *Harambee* school students passed the KJSE in five subjects (45). *Harambee* schools are largely one-stream rural schools, often self-limiting both educationally and economically; they have frequently taken over primary school buildings and reunited many of the better-qualified primary school teachers. They provide a basically academic education, the type best understood by the families which support them. The schools bear witness not only to an amazing popular faith in education, but also to a remarkable capacity on the part of peasant farmers to generate considerable amounts of capital. If the curriculum of *Harambee* schools were broadened to give more emphasis to the practical needs of rural youth, there would be a greater possibility of rewarding this faith than exists at present.

Although aided secondary schools are of considerably higher quality than the *Harambee* schools, they are equally tied to an academic curriculum and a competitive examination system. By the early 1960's, the Cambridge Overseas School Certificate, granted after four years of secondary education, had replaced the KPE as the key to most types of wage employment. The resulting anxieties of secondary school students and teachers had a profound effect on the process of education in these schools. In calling for a more imaginative kind of teaching, the Ominde Commission attacked the Cambridge School Certificate as "a real enemy, for it is entirely possible to pass in subjects merely by amassing knowledge, cramming book learning that has little educational significance in itself, except perhaps as a training of the memory (46)." In fact, the fault lay not with the Cambridge Examinations, which provided a "needed constant," but with the poor methods of teaching and learning which had developed around them. In recent years, some steps have been taken to improve the situation. In October, 1967, an act of the East African Community created the East African Examinations Council, replacing the Cambridge Certificate with the East African Certificate of Education (47). A close working relationship between the new council and the Cambridge Syndicate was established, and secondary school syllabi have gradually become more relevant to the East African situation. "English literature" now embraces the writings of Africans, and African history is taught in the third and fourth years of secondary school. The Curriculum Development and Research Center has done much to encourage new mathematics and science curriculums. For example, the Nuffield Science Teaching Project began in Britain in 1962 with the aim of presenting science in "a more lively, exciting and intelligible way (48)," and in December, 1970, the first Kenyan students sat for the Nuffield Physics School Certificate Examination. One of the main functions of Kenya Science Teachers College is to train teachers for the new science course, and a workshop course has been designed to give practice in scientific demonstration and in the use and manipulation of laboratory equipment. The changes in curricula and teacher training are designed to overcome persistent suspicion and hostility on the part of secondary school students toward departures from traditional methods.

There has been considerable discussion of the best way for secondary schools to produce "a steady and reliable supply of technologists, technicians and craftsmen . . . essential for any nation attempting to industrialize and modernize its economy (49)." In addition to Kenya Polytechnic, there were 15 technical schools in 1970. The 1970-74 Development Plan proposed to expand their combined enrollments from 4,021 in 1968 to 7,382 in 1974 (50), but few of the academic secondary schools equip their students for any skill other than simple clerical work, for which there is now little further demand. In 1960, agriculture and industrial arts were introduced at Chavakali, the first *Harambee* day secondary school in western Kenya. The project was started on a pilot basis after lengthy discussions between Ministry officials and local residents. An important step forward was the approval in 1962 by the Cambridge Syndicate of a four-year syllabus for "Agricultural Principals and Practice," and the examination was to include both written and field work (51). However, the importance attached to the creation of the syllabus suggests the difficulty of promoting any subject which cannot be offered for School Certificate. Industrial arts still lacks this status, and Chavakali has not entirely lived up to its promise of producing school leavers interested in manual work, particularly farming, and acting as catalysts for agricultural change in their neighborhoods.

Nevertheless, Chavakali represented an important breakthrough in curriculum reform in its application of the ideal of a new kind of rural school emphasizing practical subjects, and it has had a lasting effect on education in Kenya. In 1964, the Ministry of Education, with the help of an AID contract with the University of West Virginia, expanded the Vocational Agriculture program to include schools in every province. Egerton Agricultural College at Njoro began training teachers for the new course, and by 1966 nearly 1,000 students were enrolled in agriculture courses throughout the country. In the same year, the World Bank stipulated that IDA loan funds would only be available to schools teaching at least one practical subject, including domestic science and commercial subjects among the possibilities (52). Because of the great demand for intermediate-level manpower in commercial subjects, the proportion of practical subjects to academic subjects taught is gradually growing. The 1970-74 Development Plan proposed a large capital program, to be assisted by the World Bank, to construct and equip many more agricultural, home science, and industrial arts workshops and to provide equipment for teaching commercial subjects in 30 schools (53).

The Kenya Government has thus developed a definite commitment to the introduction of practical subjects into the secondary curriculum. It is still too soon to assess the impact of this. So far, few secondary students have chosen farming as a career, but this may change as nonfarm employment becomes increasingly scarce. Problems remain, particularly with relation to agriculture, which must be made to appear as a viable profit-making concern, if it is to attract many school leavers. Furthermore, the high degree of mechanization in the school agriculture program makes it very expensive to operate, and until agricultural training and other such subjects are accepted as legitimate academic subjects by the University of Nairobi, agriculture will remain a second priority for students and Government officials (54).

CHANGING PERSPECTIVES

Nearly all observers of the educational scene in Africa have been critical of the transplantation of European systems onto African soil. This criticism has focused on two main problems: the alienation of the educated minority from its traditional culture and values, and the irrelevance of an academic curriculum to the economic needs of a largely agricultural society. In Kenya, it was the Phelps-Stokes Report of 1925 which first called attention to these deficiencies.

During the 1960's Kenya chose rapid expansion of its formal school system as the path to social and economic development. Its citizens showed that they shared their Government's faith in formal education by carrying out a self-help program more widespread than that of any other African nation (55). Access to general education has been equalized to a greater extent than in many other independent African states. But the demands for high- and middle-level manpower in the modern sector of the economy have largely been met, and every year larger numbers of school leavers, both primary and secondary, are unable to obtain the urban wage employment to which they aspire. The effects of mass education on aspirations, motivations, and social attitudes are uncertain and require much more investigation. It is these questions, linked to the problem of large-scale unemployment among school leavers, which have led the Kenya Government to look for solutions outside the conventional school system.

In September, 1966, University College, Nairobi, with the full support of the Kenya Government, sponsored an international conference at Kericho, Kenya, to examine the interrelated issues of education, employment, and rural development (56). The participants were drawn from a variety of fields, including agriculture, education, economic planning, and labor relations, and they brought a broad range of perspectives to bear on the problem, emphasizing the necessity for seeing education as part of an integrated strategy in promoting rural development.

The Conference emphasized that "the path towards eventual industrialization lies through development of agriculture . . . with a constant effort to build industries on its output," and that "expenditure on bringing new knowledge to peasant farmers is probably the most productive investment which can be made in any of the poor agricultural economies (57)." The Conference also supported the belief of the Ominde Commission that primary schools could not be used successfully to train modern farmers, although they might do much to foster attitudes in sympathy with the rural environment.

Studies of school leaver attitudes presented at the Conference showed that the educated youth of Kenya were not opposed to engaging in agriculture per se, but were dissatisfied with a way of life, bound by traditional social and economic habits, and offering little financial incentive, with which farming was generally associated. Thus, in stressing the importance of agricultural education in the solution of many social, technical, and economic problems of rural Africa, V. L. Griffiths noted that "in backward rural areas the schools cannot be made a main instrument of economic progress. . . . Only when economic development is already taking place can the schools be expected to play any part—and then it will be an important but subsidiary part (58)."

Although the main theme of the Conference was the so-called primary school leaver problem, discussion made it clear that the school leaver could only be considered within a broader perspective of the entire rural environment. The Conference generally concluded that the most urgent educational need lay outside the formal school system and that adult education offered the greatest potential for providing productive employment for the majority, whether literate or illiterate; the participants were not in full agreement, however, on specific proposals regarding out-of-school training. They also recognized that the Government's continued commitment to the rapid expansion of the school system severely limited the financial resources available for any new approaches, and agreed on the need for such approaches to have low unit costs and on the importance of redirecting the impressive popular enthusiasm for education away from its academic orientation towards a more practical, rurally-oriented curriculum. Despite the problems involved in finding a solution to the questions it raised, the Kericho Conference did offer a new perspective on rural transformation.

Since Independence, the Government of Kenya has demonstrated its concern for the slow rate of rural development and the growing unemployment of school leavers through the creation of a number of new training programs, both for adults and for youth. Kenya has an impressive network of agricultural training facilities, based on the infrastructure developed by and for the European settler-farmers, including its railroad system and the experimental stations for agricultural research. These facilities range from Egerton College, which trains agricultural specialists to diploma level, and Farmer Training Centers offering short intensive courses to peasant farmers, to an agricultural extension embracing a wide variety of advisory services, but both the extension and the Training Centers serve primarily those farmers who are already the most progressive in the country. The Training Centers have been particularly successful in promoting progressive farming practices, but they have devoted a great deal of time to teaching government agricultural officials, have poor staff morale, and could greatly expand their advisory services to farmers (59). Basic agricultural training for young people has mainly been channeled through 4-K Clubs, rural extension clubs modeled on the American 4-H system, and linked to the primary schools (60). In addition, Kenya's National Youth Service has offered a wide range of vocational education to more than 7,000 youths. Many of these young people have found jobs, but per capita training costs are too high to permit large-scale expansion of this program.

Until 1966, the different programs in out-of-school education were run independent of each other by a number of Government ministries, in addition to those sponsored by voluntary agencies. In 1966, the Government established the Board of Adult Education, with responsibility for planning and coordinating all activities in this sphere (61). The Board can integrate the many elements within each district which provide adult education, thus minimizing wasteful competition and overlapping. To translate a national plan into action at the local level, the Government hoped that the adult education supervisors would participate in the proposed development advisory committees at district level, where available facilities could be efficiently utilized as "multi-purpose training centers." This was in line with the recommendations of the Kericho Conference and reflected the Government's support of the overall conclusions of the Conference in the 1970-74 Development Plan (62).

Following the Kericho Conference, concern for the role of education in rural development was voiced in many other quarters. Within Kenya, the churches reported on the growing unemployment of untrained primary school leavers, and proposed the establishment of village polytechnics as low-cost centers providing training in such essential skills as carpentry and building (63). The 1968 UNESCO Conference, in stressing quality rather than quantity education, recommended that the primary school should inculcate a greater respect for manual work and that all education should be integrated within a plan geared to rural development (64). A number of international aid organizations, most notably the World Bank, have also begun to stress the need for more investment in "non-formal" education, tied to rural employment and development. This reflects a growing disillusionment with the economically unproductive expansion of formal schools in Africa.

The 1970-74 Kenya Development Plan reiterated these concerns insofar as it emphasized "the strategy of rural development as the route of national development (65)." The Plan accepted the conclusions of the Kericho Conference that "co-ordinated local development to yield higher incomes and more employment opportunities for youth is of the highest priority," and proposed a Special Rural Development Program through pilot projects in 14 selected areas (66). The Plan also expressed interest in new possibilities such as village polytechnics as part of its concern with the provision of increased training for adults within the rural development program.

It is too early to assess the impact of the proposals in the 1970-74 Development Plan. Expansion of the formal school system is continuing, resulting in a lack of resources which has made it difficult for the

Government to embark on other new programs. Popular pressure for more academic schooling will probably continue, and "practical" education will remain a second choice until there is more evidence that it can be profitable in terms of finding jobs. The recurring calls for "adaptation" in African education are reminiscent of the recommendations of the Phelps-Stokes Commission in the 1920's. The difference is that a solution can no longer be imposed from outside. Kenya now faces the challenge of developing a system of education uniquely suited to her own national political, social, and economic needs.

Notes

1. Kenya African National Union, *What a KANU Government Offers You,* (Nairobi: Press and Publicity Dept., KANU, 1963), p. 4.

2. The Commission was headed by Professor-elect of the University College, Dr. Simeon Ominde, and included Jeremiah Nyagah, A. J. Pandya, J. K. Ndile, T. Towett, Mohamed Hyder, J. B. Wambugu, Mrs. Ruth Habwe, Joab Ochieng, T. Lung'aho, Alderman I. Somen, and P. Fordham. "Six-Year Plan," *Reporter*, III, no. 101 (February 24, 1964), 29.

3. *Kenya Education Commission Report* (Ominde Report), Part I (Nairobi: Government Printer, 1964), p. 10.

4. *Ibid.,* p. 29.

5. *Ibid.,* p. 22.

6. *Ibid.,* p. 29.

7. *Ibid.,* p. 23.

8. *Ibid.,* pp. 60-61.

9. Kenya Government, Ministry of Economic Planning and Development, *High-Level Manpower Requirements and Resources in Kenya 1964-70* (Nairobi: Government Printer, May, 1965), pp. 41-42.

10. Ominde Report, Part I, p. 56.

11. In 1965 there were 150 unaided schools (mainly *Harambee*) and by 1966 over half of Kenya's secondary schools were unaided, providing for a third of the total number of secondary students. Ministry of Education, *Triennial Survey 1964-66* (Nairobi: Government Printer, 1967), p. 21.

12. Kenya Government, *Development Plan 1964-70,* (Nairobi: Government Printer, 1964), pp. 102-104.

13. Ominde Report, Part II, (1965), p. 24. Form I enrollment in public secondary schools as a percentage of KPE entries in the previous year dropped from 14.4 percent in 1964 to 10.6 percent in 1965.

14. *Ibid.,* pp. 21-25.

15. See John Anderson, "The Kenya Education Commission Report: An African View of Educational Planning," *Comparative Education Review*, IX, no. 2 (June, 1965), 201-207.

16. Weeks, *Divergence in Educational Development: The Case of Kenya and Uganda*, p. 23.

17. Ernest Stabler, *Education Since Uhuru: The Schools of Kenya* (Middletown, Connecticut: Wesleyan University Press, 1969), p. 165.

18. Weeks, *op. cit.*, p. 20. Kenya's long-awaited White Paper on education was redrafted several times but has never been approved.

19. *UNESCO Conference on Education and Scientific and Technical Training in Relation to Development in Africa*, Nairobi, July, 1968. Final Report (Paris: UNESCO, 1968), p. 8.

20. Weeks, *op. cit.*, p. 11.

21. Kenya Government, *Development Plan 1970-74* (Nairobi: Government Printer, 1969), pp. 453-454.

22. Kenya Ministry of Education, *Annual Report, 1969*, p. 4. Between 1968 and 1969 primary enrollment increased by six percent, the rate which the plan proposes to maintain.

23. Kenya Government, *Development Plan 1966-1970* (Nairobi: Government Printer, 1966), p. 310.

24. Kenya Government, *Development Plan 1970-74*, pp. 454-5.

25. Kenya Government, *The Teachers Service Commission Act, 1966*, no. 2 of 1967, p. 3.

26. Kenya Government, *Development Plan 1970-74*, p. 456.

27. *Report of the Conference on the Review of the Educational System in Eastern Nigeria* (Enugu: Government Printer, 1964), p. 1. See also David Abernathy, *The Political Dilemma of Popular Education; An African Case* (Stanford, California: Stanford University Press, 1969).

28. Kenya Government, *Development Plan 1970-74*, p. 459-60.

29. Kenya Ministry of Education, *Annual Report 1971*, pp. 45, 55.

30. Lewis Brownstein, "Preliminary Results of a Survey of 1964 K. P. E. Candidates in Embu, Kitui, Kericho and Nyanza." Discussion paper no. 58, Institute for Development Studies, University College, Nairobi, 1969, unpublished, p. 11.

31. Ominde Report, Part I, p. 73.

32. Kenya Ministry of Education, *Annual Report, 1965*, p. 6.

33. By 1969, 81 such schools were receiving financial aid from the Government and in 1969 alone the Government opened a total of 34 new Form I streams.

34. Stabler, *op. cit.*, pp. 86, 96-102.

35. Edwin Williams, "A Historiographical Review of the Writings of Terence Ranger of East, Central and South Africa," January, 1969, unpublished, p. 2. For a more critical analysis see Donald Denoon and Adam Kuper, "The New Historiography in Dar es Salaam," *African Affairs*, LXIX, no. 277 (October, 1970), 329-349.

36. Kenya Government, *Development Plan 1966-1970*, p. 311.

37. Stabler, *op. cit.*, p. 137.

38. Kenya Ministry of Education, *Triennial Survey 1964-66*, p. 50, and *Annual Report, 1970*, p. 88.

39. Kyale Mwendwa, "Kenya Institute of Education," *Teacher Education Bulletin* (Nairobi: Equatorial Publishers, 1967), p. 30.

40. Kenya Ministry of Education, *Triennial Survey 1964-66*, pp. 26-27.

41. *Ibid.*, p. 5.

42. L. Gray Cowan, *The Cost of Learning: The Politics of Primary Education in Kenya* (New York: Teachers College Press, 1970), p. 30.

43. Quoted in Stabler, *op. cit.*, p. 28.

44. John Anderson, "Report on the Conference of Harambee School Headmasters," August, 1966, paper prepared for the Department of Education, University College, Nairobi, mimeo.

45. Stabler, *op. cit.*, p. 163.

46. Ominde Report, Part I, p. 69.

47. Kenya Ministry of Education, *Annual Report, 1967*, p. 16.

48. Stabler, *op. cit.*, p. 80.

49. Kenya Government, *Development Plan 1970-74*, p. 462.

50. *Ibid.*, pp. 462-465.

51. Robert Maxwell, "Teaching Agriculture in Secondary Schools," *East Africa Journal* (June, 1965), pp. 27-28.

52. Kenya Ministry of Education, *Triennial Survey 1964-66*, p. 7.

53. *Kenya Development Plan 1970-74*, p. 460.

54. Jon Moris, "Education and Training of the Farmer," paper presented at the Conference on Education, Employment and Rural Development, Kericho, Kenya, September, 1966, unpublished, pp. E9-E12.

55. African Socialism in Kenya has been translated into educational policy aimed at equal opportunity for all. Kenya, *African Socialism and Its Application to Planning in Kenya.* Sessional Paper, no. 10 of 1965 (Nairobi: Government Printer, 1965).

56. James R. Sheffield (ed.), *Education, Employment and Rural Development,* Report of the Kericho (Kenya) Conference 25th September-1st October, 1966, (Nairobi: East African Publishing House, 1967).

57. Guy Hunter, "Education, Employment and Rural Development: The Problem in East Africa," in Sheffield (ed.), *Education, Employment and Rural Development,* p. 38.

58. V. L. Griffiths, "The Education of the Young in Rural Areas," in Sheffield (ed.), *Education, Employment and Rural Development,* p. 307. See also the summary of the Griffiths Report in Chapter VI, and Phillip Foster, "The Vocational School Fallacy in Development

Planning," in Mary Jean Bowman, *Readings in the Economics of Education* (UNESCO: Paris, 1968).

59. Kenya Government, *Report of the Agricultural Education Commission,* (Nairobi: Government Printer, 1967). The best analyses of the rule of the FTCs and extension services are contained in "Issues in Rural Development in Kenya," by P. M. Mbithi, and "Does Extension Create Poverty in Kenya?" by Joseph Ascroft et. al. in *East Africa Journal,* IX, no. 3 (March, 1972).

60. The 4 Ks are *Kuugana* (to unite), *Kufanya* (to work), *Kusaidia* (to help), and Kenya.

61. Kenya Gazette Supplement no. 15, Acts 1966, "The Board of Adult Education Act, 1966," (Nairobi: Government Printer, 1966).

62. For a description of the proposed role of the Board of Education, see Paul Fordham and J. R. Sheffield, "Continuing Education for Youth and Adults" and "Conference Conclusions," Numbers 70-77 in Sheffield (ed.), *Education, Employment and Rural Development.*

63. *After School What?* A report prepared by a joint working party of the Youth Department of the Christian Council of Kenya and the Christian Churches Educational Association (Nairobi: Ministry of Health, 1966).

64. UNESCO Conference on Education and Scientific and Technical Training in Relation to Development in Africa, final report (Paris, 1964).

65. Kenya Government, *Development Plan 1970-74*, p. 166.

66. *Ibid.*, pp. 174-75.

Bibliography

PRIMARY SOURCES

Government Reports

East Africa. *Report of the Working Party on Higher Education in East Africa.* Nairobi: Government Printer, 1958.

East African Governors' Conference. *Technical Education and Vocational Training in East Africa.* London: Crown Agents for the Colonies, 1948.

East African Protectorate. *Correspondence Relating to the Masai.* London: O.H.M.S., Cmd. 5584 of 1911.

_____. *Education Report, 1909.* Nairobi: Government Printer, 1909.

_____. *Evidence of the Education Commission, 1919.* Nairobi: The Swift Press, 1919.

Great Britain, Colonial Office. *A Survey of Vocational-Technical Education in the Colonial Empire.* Col. No. 177. London: H.M.S.O., 1940.

_____. *East Africa: Report of the Economic and Fiscal Commission.* Cmd. 1279. London: H.M.S.O., 1961.

_____. *Higher Education in East Africa.* Col. No. 142. London: H.M.S.O., 1937. (The de la Warr Commission.)

_____. *Indians in Kenya.* Cmd. 1922. London: H.M.S.O., 1923. (The Devonshire White Paper.)

_____. *Kenya: Independence Conference, 1963.* Cmd. 2156. London: H.M.S.O., 1963.

_____. *Memorandum on Mass Education in African Society.* Col. No. 186. London: H.M.S.O., 1943.

_____. *Kenya: Proposals for a Reconstruction of the Government.* Cmd. 9103. London: H.M.S.O., March, 1954. (The Lyttleton Constitution.)

_____. *Kenya: Proposals for New Constitutional Arrangements.* Cmd. 309. London: H.M.S.O., 1957.

——————. *Report of the Kenya Constitutional Conference.* Cmd. 960. London: H.M.S.O., February, 1960. (The Lancaster House Conference.)

——————. *Report of the Kenya Conference, 1962.* Cmd. 1700. London: H.M.S.O., 1962.

Great Britain, Colonial Office Advisory Committee for Education in the Colonies. *Education for Citizenship.* Col. No. 216. London: H.M.S.O., 1948.

——————. *Memorandum on the Education of African Communities.* Col. No. 103. London: H.M.S.O., 1935.

——————. *Memorandum on Native Policy in East Africa.* Cmd. 3573. London: H.M.S.O., 1930. (The Passfield White Paper.)

Great Britain, Colonial Office Advisory Committee on Native Education in the British Tropical African Dependencies. *Education Policy in British Tropical Africa.* Cmd. 2374. London: H.M.S.O., 1925.

Higher Education in East Africa. Entebbe: Government Printer, 1958. Published by joint authority of the Governments of Kenya, Tanganyika and Uganda.

Kenya Colony and Protectorate. *African Education in Kenya.* Nairobi: Government Printer, 1949. (The Beecher Report.)

——————. *A Plan to Intensify the Development of African Agriculture in Kenya.* Nairobi: Government Printer, 1954. (The Swynnerton Plan.)

——————. *A Ten-Year Plan for the Development of African Education.* Nairobi: Government Printer, 1948. (Ten-Year Plan.)

——————. *Education Department Annual Reports.* Nairobi: Government Printer (annual, 1926-1962).

——————. *Legislative Council Reports.* 1950-62.

——————. Ministry of Agriculture, Animal Husbandry and Water Resources. *African Land Development in Kenya, 1946-55.* Nairobi: Government Printer, 1956.

——————. *Report of the Teachers' Salaries Commission.* Nairobi: Government Printer, 1961.

——————. Sessional Paper No. 1 of 1950. *Proposals for the Implementation of the Recommendations of the Report on African Education in Kenya.* Nairobi: Government Printer, 1950.

——————. *Sessional Paper Number 77 of 1956/57: The Development Programme 1957/60.* Nairobi: Government Printer, 1957.

——————. *Some Aspects of the Development of Kenya Government Services for the Benefit of Africans From 1946 Onwards.* Nairobi: Government Printer, 1953.

Kenya Government. *African Socialism and its Application to Planning in Kenya.* Nairobi: Government Printer, 1965.

_____. *Development Plan 1964-70.* Nairobi: Government Printer, 1964.

_____. *Development Plan 1966-70.* Nairobi: Government Printer, 1966.

_____. *Development Plan 1970-74.* Nairobi: Government Printer, 1969.

_____. Ministry of Economic Planning and Development. *High-Level Manpower Requirements and Resources in Kenya, 1964-70.* Nairobi: Government Printer, 1965.

_____. *Report of the Agricultural Education Commission.* Nairobi: Government Printer, 1969.

_____. *Report of the Education Commission.* Nairobi: Government Printer, Part I, 1964, Part II, 1965. (Ominde Report.)

_____. Ministry of Education. *Annual Reports, 1963-1971.* Nairobi: Government Printer.

_____. Ministry of Education. *Triennial Surveys.* Nairobi: Government Printer (occasional).

_____. *Teachers Service Commission Act, 1966* (no. 2). Nairobi: Government Printer, 1967.

Nigeria Federal Ministry of Education. *Investment in Education: The Report of the Commission on Pre-School Certificate and Higher Education in Nigeria.* Lagos: Government Printer, 1960. (The Ashby Report.)

Nigeria Ministry of Education for the Eastern Region. *Report of the Conference on the Review of the Educational System in Eastern Nigeria.* Enugu: Government Printer, 1964.

Nyerere, Julius K. *Education for Self-Reliance.* Dar es Salaam: Government Printer, 1967.

United Kingdom, Central Office of Information. *Education in the United Kingdom Dependencies.* Revised 1959. London: H.M.S.O., 1959.

Other Documents

After School What? A report prepared by a joint workshop party of the Youth Department of the Christian Council of Kenya and the Christian Churches Educational Association. Nairobi: Ministry of Health, 1966.

American Council on Education, Africa Liaison Committee. *Report of Conference on Education in East Africa.* Princeton, N.J.: December, 1960. (The Princeton Conference.)

Anderson, C. Arnold. "Education in Kenya, 1961-67." Unpublished report prepared for the World Bank Report, 1961. (Mimeographed.)

Anderson, John. *Report on the Conference of Harambee Schools' Head-masters, August 1966.* A paper prepared for the Department of Education, University College, Nairobi. (Mimeographed.)

Carnegie Corporation of New York. *Village Education in Africa.* Report of the Inter-Territorial "Jeanes" Conference, Southern Rhodesia, May 27-June 6, 1935. Lovedale, South Africa: Lovedale Press, 1935.

Conference on the Development of Higher Education in Africa, Tananarive, Malagasy Republic, 1962. *Development of Higher Education in Africa.* Report of the Conference . . . 3-12 September, 1962. Paris: UNESCO, 1963. (Tananarive Report.)

Griffiths, V. L. "Some Suggestions For an African Government's Educational Policy in Kenya." Oxford, 1962. (Typewritten.)

International Bank for Reconstruction and Development. *The Economic Development of Kenya.* Baltimore: Johns Hopkins Press, 1963. (World Bank Survey.)

Nuffield Foundation and Colonial Office. *African Education: A Study of Educational Policy and Practice in British Tropical Areas.* Oxford: Oxford University Press, 1953.

Sheffield, James R. (ed.). *Education, Employment and Rural Development.* Report of the Kericho (Kenya) Conference, September, 1966. Nairobi: East African Publishing House, 1967.

United Nations Economic and Social Council. *Educational Development in Africa: Implementation of the Addis Ababa Plan.* Economic Commission for Africa. Leopoldville: February, March, 1963.

United Nations Economic Commission for Africa, Unesco. *Final Report: Conference of African States on the Development of Education in Africa.* Addis Ababa, 15-25 May, 1961. (Addis Ababa Report.)

UNESCO. *Elements of Educational Planning.* Educational Studies and Documents, No. 45. Paris: UNESCO, 1963.

UNESCO. *Meeting of Ministers of Education of African Countries Participating in the Implementation of the Addis Ababa Plan.* Paris: UNESCO, March 26-30, 1962.

SECONDARY SOURCES

Books

Abernethy, David B. *The Political Dilemma of Popular Education; An African Case.* Stanford, California: Stanford University Press, 1969.

Allport, Gordon W. *The Nature of Prejudice.* New York: Doubleday, 1954.

Almond, Gabriel A. and Coleman, James S. (eas.). *The Politics of Developing Areas*. Princeton: Princeton University Press, 1960.

Anderson, John. *The Struggle for the School*. London: Longmans, 1970.

Barnett, Donald L. and Njama, Karani. *Mau Mau From Within*. New York: Monthly Review, 1967.

Barrett, David B. *Schism and Renewal in Africa: An Analysis of Six Thousand Contemporary Religious Movements*. Nairobi: Oxford University Press, 1968.

Bascom, William R. and Herskovits, M. J. (eds.). *Continuity and Change in African Cultures*. Chicago: University of Chicago Press, 1958.

Battuta, Ibn. *Travels in Asia and Africa*. Trans. H.A.R. Gibb. London: Routledge, 1929.

Bennett, George. *Kenya: A Political History: The Colonial Period*. Oxford University Press, 1963.

Biesheuvel, S. *African Intelligence*. Johannesburg: South African Institute of Race Relations, 1943.

————. *Race, Culture and Personality*. Johannesburg: South African Institute of Race Relations, 1959.

Black, Eugene R. *The Diplomacy of Economic Development and Other Papers*. New York: Atheneum, 1963.

Blood, A. G. (ed.). *The Fortunate Few*. London: Universities Mission to Central Africa, 1954.

Bromhead, Walter S. *What's What in the Kenya Highlands; Their Pioneering Romance and Colonizing Possibilities*. Nairobi: East African Standard, 1924.

Buell, R. L. *The Native Problem in Africa*. (Two vols.) London: Macmillan, 1928.

Burns, Donald G. *African Education: An Introductory Survey of Education in Commonwealth Countries*. London: Oxford University Press, 1965.

Butts, R. Freeman. *American Education in International Development*. New York: Harper and Row, 1963.

Cameron, Sir Donald. *My Tanganyika Service and Some Nigeria*. London: Allen and Unwin, 1939.

Campbell, John McLeod. *African History in the Making*. London: Edinburgh House Press, 1956.

Carey-Jones, N. S. *The Anatomy of A Human*. New York: Praeger, 1969.

Carothers, J. C. *The Psychology of Mau Mau*. Nairobi: Government Printer, 1954.

Carr-Saunders, Sir Alexander. *Staffing African Universities*. London: Overseas Development Institute, 1963.

Castle, E. B. *Growing Up in East Africa*. London: Oxford University Press, 1966.

Cell, John W. *British Colonial Administration in the Mid-Nineteenth Century: The Policy-Making Process.* New Haven: Yale University Press, 1970.

Clarke, P. J., *A Short History of Tanganyika.* London: Longmans, 1960.

Cohen, Sir Andrew. *British Policy in Changing Africa.* Evanston: Northwestern University Press, 1959.

Coleman, James S. (ed.). *Education and Political Development.* Princeton: Princeton University Press, 1965.

Corfield, F. D. *Historical Survey of the Origins and Growth of Mau Mau.* London: H.M.S.O., 1960.

Coupland, Reginald. *East Africa and Its Invaders.* Oxford: Clarendon Press, 1938.

Cowan, L. Gray. *The Cost of Learning: The Politics of Primary Education in Kenya.* New York: Teachers College Press, 1970.

Curle, Adam. *Educational Strategy for Developing Societies.* London: Tavistock Publications, 1963.

Delf, G. *Asians in East Africa.* London: Oxford University Press, 1963.

Dilley, Margery R. *British Policy in Kenya Colony.* New York: Nelson, 1937.

Dodd, William A. *"Education for Self-Reliance" in Tanzania: A Study of its Vocational Aspects.* New York: Teachers College Press, 1969.

Doob, Leonard W. *Becoming More Civilized: A Psychological Exploration.* New Haven: Yale University Press, 1960.

Dougall, James W. C. (ed.). *A Village Teacher's Guide.* London: The Sheldon Press, 1931.

—————. *Missionary Education in Kenya and Uganda, A Study of Cooperation.* London: International Missionary Council, 1936.

Eliot, Sir Charles. *The British East Africa Protectorate.* London: Arnold, 1905.

Elvin, Lionel. *Education and the End of Empire.* University of London Institute of Education. Studies in Education No. 8. London: Evans Brothers, 1956.

Emerson, Rupert. *From Empire to Nation.* Cambridge: Harvard University Press, 1960.

Fallers, Lloyd. *Bantu Bureaucracy.* Cambridge, England: Heffer for the East African Institute of Social Research, 1955.

Farson, Negley. *Last Chance in Africa.* London: Victor Gollancz Ltd., 1949.

Forde, C. Daryll (ed.). *African Worlds.* London: Oxford University Press, 1954.

—————. (ed.). *Social Implications of Industrialism and Urbanization in Africa South of the Sahara.* Paris: UNESCO, 1956.

Forrester, Marion W. *Kenya To-Day: Social Prerequisites for Economic Development.* Gravenhage, Netherlands: Mouton and Co., 1962.

Foster, George M. *Traditional Cultures, And the Impact of Technological Change.* New York: Harper and Row, 1962.

Frankel, S. Herbert. *The Economic Impact on Underdeveloped Societies.* Cambridge: Harvard University Press, 1953.

Frager, J. Nelson. *Report on Education in the East African Protectorate.* Nairobi: The East African Leader Office, 1909.

Freeman-Grenville, G. *The East African Coast.* London: Oxford University Press, 1963.

Geertz, Clifford (ed.). *Old Societies and New States.* Glencoe: Free Press, 1963.

George, Betty. *Education for Africans in Tanganyika.* U.S. Office of Education, Bulletin 1960, No. 19. Washington: Government Printing Office, 1960.

Goldthorpe, John. *Outlines of East African Society.* Kampala: Department of Sociology, Makerere University College, 1959.

Ghai, D. P. *Portrait of a Minority.* London: Oxford University Press, 1965.

Gregory, J. W. *The Foundation of British East Africa.* New York: Negro Universities Press, 1969. (First published in 1901.)

Groves, C. P. *The Planting of Christianity in Africa, vols. I-IV.* London: Lutterworth Press, 1948-1964.

Gulliver, P. H. *Social Control in an African Society: The Agricultural Masai of Northern Tanganyika.* Boston: Boston University Press, 1963.

Gutkind and Southall. *Townsmen in the Making.* East African Institute for Social Research, 1958.

Hagen, Everett E. *On the Theory of Social Change.* Homewood: The Dorsey Press, 1962.

Hailey, Lord. *An African Survey, Revised 1956.* London: Oxford University Press, 1957.

Harbison, Frederick and Myers, Charles A. *Education, Manpower and Economic Growth: Strategies of Human Resource Development.* New York: McGraw-Hill Book Company, 1964.

Hardinge, Sir A. H. *A Diplomatist in the East.* London: Cape, 1928.

Harlan, Vincent and Chilver, E. M. (eds.). *History of East Africa, vol. II.* Oxford: Clarendon Press, 1965.

Herskovits, Melville. *The Human Factor in Changing Africa.* New York: Knopf, 1962.

Hill, M. F. *Permanent Way.* Nairobi: E. A. Railways and Harbours, 1950.

Hobley, C. W. *Kenya from Chartered Company to Crown Colony.* London: Witherby, 1929.

Hodgkin, Robin A. *Education and Change.* London: Oxford University Press, 1957.

Hodgkin, Thomas. *Nationalism in Colonial Africa*. New York: New York University Press, 1957.

Hughes, A. J. *East Africa: The Search For Unity*. Baltimore: Penguin Books, 1963.

Hunter, Guy. *The Best of Both Worlds*. London: Oxford University Press, 1967.

_____. *Education For A Developing Region*. London: Allen and Unwin, 1963.

_____. *The New Societies of Tropical Africa*. London: Oxford University Press, 1962.

Huxley, Elspeth. *White Man's Country: Lord Delamere and the Making of Kenya*. Two vols. London: Chatto and Windus, 1935.

_____, and Perham, Margery. *Race and Politics in Kenya*. New and revised edition. London: Faber and Faber, Ltd., 1955.

Ingham, Kenneth. *A History of East Africa*. London: Longmans, 1962.

_____. *The Making of Modern Uganda*. London: Allen and Unwin, 1957.

Jackson, Sir Frederick. *Early Days in East Africa*. London: Arnold and Company, 1930.

Jeffries, Sir Charles. *Transfer of Power*. London: Pall Mall Press, 1960.

Jones, Lance G. E. *The Jeanes Teacher in the United States, 1908-1933: An Account of Twenty-five Years Experiment in the Supervision of Negro Rural Schools*. Chapel Hill: University of North Carolina Press, 1937.

Jones, Thomas Jesse. *Education in East Africa*. London: Edinburgh House Press, 1925.

Kariuki, Josiah M. *Mau Mau Detainee*. London: Oxford University Press, 1963.

Kenyatta, Jomo. *Facing Mount Kenya*. New York: Vintage, 1962.

Kimambo, I., and Temu, A. J. (eds.). *A History of Tanzania*. Nairobi: East African Publishing House, 1969.

Kitchen, Helen (ed.). *The Educated African*. New York: Praeger, 1962.

Koinange, Mbiyu. *The People of Kenya Speak for Themselves*. Detroit: Kenya Publications Fund, 1955.

Krapf, Ludwig. *Travels, Researches and Missionaries Labours During an 18 Years Residence in Eastern Africa*. London: Tribner and Col, 1860.

Laye, Camara. *The Dark Child*. New York: Noonday Press, 1954.

Leakey, L. S. B. *Defeating Mau Mau*. London: Methuen, 1954.

_____. *Mau Mau and the Kikuyu*. London: Methuen, 1952.

_____. *The Progress and Evolution of Man in Africa*. London: Oxford University Press, 1961.

Lerner, Daniel. *The Passing of Traditional Society*. Glencoe: The Free Press, 1958.

Lewis, L. J. *Educational Policy and Practice in British Tropical Areas*. London: Thomas Nelson and Sons, Ltd., 1954.

_____. *Partnership in Overseas Education*. Studies in Education Number 9. London: Evans Brothers, Ltd., 1959.

_____. *Perspectives in Mass Education and Community Development*. London: Thomas Nelson and Sons, Ltd., 1955.

_____ (ed.). *The Phelps-Stokes Reports on Education in Africa*. Abridged. London: Oxford University Press, 1962.

Leys, Norman. *The Colour Bar in East Africa*. London: Hogarth Press, 1941.

Lucas, Eric. *English Traditions in East African Education*. London: Oxford University Press, 1959.

Lugard, Sir Frederick Dealtry. *The Rise of Our East African Empire*. Vols. I and II. Edinburgh and London: Blackwood, 1926.

Mair, Lucy. *New Nations*. Chicago: University of Chicago Press, 1963.

_____. *Primitive Government*. New York: Penguin, 1962.

Mason, Reginald J. *British Education in Africa*. London: Oxford University Press, 1959.

Maunier, Rene. *The Sociology of Colonies*. E. O. Lorimer, ed. and translator. Vol. I. London: Routledge and K. Paul, 1949.

Mayhew, Arthur. *Education in the Colonial Empire*. London: Longmans, 1938.

Mboya, Tom. *Freedom and After*. Boston: Little, Brown and Co., 1963.

McKay, Vernon. *Africa in World Politics*. New York: Harper and Row, 1963.

Meinertzhagen, R. *Kenya Diary, 1902-1906*. Edinburgh: Oliver and Boyd, 1957.

Millikan, Max F., and Blackmer, Donald C. M. (eds.). *The Emerging Nations*. Boston: Little, Brown and Co., 1961.

Mitchell, Sir Philip. "Africa and The West in Historical Perspective," *Africa Today*. C. Grove Haines, ed. Baltimore: Johns Hopkins Press, 1955.

_____. *The Agrarian Problem in Kenya*. Nairobi: Government Printer, 1948.

Mungean, G. H. *British Rule in Kenya 1895-1912: The Establishment of Administration in the East Africa Protectorate*. Oxford: Clarendon Press, 1966.

Murray, A. Victor. *The School in the Bush*. London: Longmans, Green and Company, 1929.

Neil, Bishop S. *A History of Christian Missions*. London: Penguin Books, 1969.

Odinga, Oginga. *Not Yet Uhuru: An Autobiography.* London: Heinemann, 1969.

Ogot, B. A., and Kieran, J. A. (eds.). *Zamani: A Survey of East African History.* Nairobi: East African Publishing House, 1968.

Oldham, J. H., and Gibson, B. D. *The Remaking of Man in Africa.* London: Oxford University Press, 1931.

Oliver, Lord. *White Capital and Coloured Labour.* London: Hogarth Press, 1929.

Oliver, Roland A. *The Missionary Factor in East Africa.* London: Longmans, Green and Company, 1952.

——————, and Mathew, Gervase (eds.). *History of East Africa.* Vol. I. London: Oxford University Press, 1963.

Ottenberg, Simon and Phoebe (eds.). *Cultures and Societies of Africa.* New York: Random House, 1960.

Patterson, J. H. *The Man-Eaters of Tsavo and Other East African Adventures.* London: Macmillan, 1907.

Perham, Margery. *The Colonial Reckoning.* New York: Knopf, 1962.

Philip, Horace R. *A New Day in Kenya.* London, New York: World Dominion Press, 1936.

Pifer, Alan J. "Education: Bulwark of Nigerian Independence." *Africa in Transition.* The Kennecott Lecture Series, 1960-61, No. 6. Tucson: University of Arizona Press, 1961.

Plamenatz, John. *Alien Rule and Self-Government.* London: Longmans, Green and Company, 1960.

Porter, J. C. "Adult Education at the Jeanes School for Community Development in Kenya." *Yearbook of Education 1954.* London: Evans Brothers, Ltd., 1954.

Pye, Lucian W. *Politics, Personality and Nation-Building: Burma's Search For Identity.* New Haven: Yale University Press, 1962.

Ranger, T. *Emerging Themes in African History.* Nairobi: East African Publishing House, 1968.

——————. *Aspects of Central African History.* London: Heinemann, 1968.

Read, Margaret. *Education and Cultural Traditions.* University of London; Institute of Education, Studies in Education, No. 2. London: University of London, 1950.

——————. *Education and Social Change in Tropical Areas.* London: Thomas Nelson and Sons, Ltd., 1955.

Richards, A. I. (ed.). *East African Chiefs.* London: Faber and Faber, for the East African Institute of Social Research, 1960.

Robinson, R., and Gallagher, J. *Africa and the Victorians.* London: Macmillan and Co., 1961.

Rosberg, Carl G., Jr., and Nottingham, John. *The Myth of Mau Mau: Nationalism in Kenya.* New York: Praeger, 1966.

Rosberg, Carl G., Jr. "Political Conflict and Change in Kenya," in *Transition in Africa, Studies in Political Adaptation.* G. M. Carter and W. O. Brown, eds. African Research Studies, No. 1. Boston: Boston University, 1958.

——————, and Bennett, George. *The Kenyatta Election.* London: Oxford University Press, 1961.

Ross, W. Macgregor. *Kenya From Within.* London: Allen and Unwin, 1927.

Rostow, W. W. *The Stages of Economic Growth.* London: Cambridge University Press, 1960.

Rothchild, Donald S. *Toward Unity in Africa.* Washington: Public Affairs Press, 1960.

——————. *The Politics of Integration.* Nairobi: East African Publishing House, 1968.

Scanlon, David G. *Education in Uganda.* Washington: Government Printing Office, 1964.

——————. *International Education: A Documentary History.* New York: Teachers College Press, 1960.

Shepherd, George, Jr. *The Politics of African Nationalism.* New York: Praeger, 1962.

Shields, James J., Jr. *A Selected Bibliography on Education in East Africa: 1941-1961.* Kampala: Makerere University Press, 1962.

Shields, James J., Jr. *The Reports of the Phelps-Stokes Fund on Education in Africa and the Foundation of a Theory of Community Development by the British.* New York: Phelps-Stokes Fund Occasional Paper Number 4, May 4, 1961.

Slater, Montagu. *The Trial of Jomo Kenyatta.* 2nd ed. rev. London: Secker and Warburg, 1957.

Smith, Rev. Edwin W. (ed.). *African Ideas of God.* London: Edinburgh House Press, 1950.

——————. *The Christian Mission in Africa.* London: Edinburgh House Press, 1926.

Somerset, H. C. A. *Predicting Success in School Certificate.* Nairobi: East African Publishing House, 1968.

Southall, Aidan (ed.). *Social Change in Modern Africa.* London: Oxford University Press, 1961.

Stabler, Ernest. *Education Since Uhuru: The Schools of Kenya.* Middletown, Connecticut: Wesleyan University Press, 1969.

Strandes, J. *The Portuguese Period in East Africa.* Translated by Jean Wallwork. Nairobi: Kenya Historical Society, 1961.

Vaizey, John. *The Economics of Education.* New York: The Free Press of Glencoe, Inc., 1962.

Wallerstein, Immanuel. *The Politics of Independence.* New York: Vintage, 1961.

Weeks, Sheldon. *Divergence in Educational Development: The Case of Kenya and Uganda.* New York: Teachers College Press, 1967.

Welbourn, F. B. *East African Rebels: A Study of Some Independent Churches.* London: S. C. M. Press, 1961.

Welbourn, F. B., and Ogot, B. A. *A Place to Feel at Home.* London: Oxford University Press, 1966.

Wood, A. W. *Vocational and Social Training of Primary School Leavers in the African Countries of the Commonwealth.* London: Commonwealth Secretariat, 1969.

Wood, Susan. *Kenya: The Tensions of Progress.* London Institute of Race Relations: Oxford University Press, 1961.

Wraith, Ronald E. *East African Citizen.* New York: Oxford University Press, 1960.

Periodicals

"African Education in Kenya: The Beecher Report," *Times Educational Supplement,* no. 1852 (October 27, 1950), 821.

Anderson, John. "The Kenya Education Commission Report: An African View of Educational Planning." *Comparative Education Review,* IX, no. 2 (June, 1965), 201-207.

———. "Self-Help and Independency: The Political Implications of a Continuing Tradition in African Education in Kenya," *African Affairs,* LXX, no. 278 (January, 1971).

Beecher, L. J. "Missionary Education in Kenya," *The East and the West,* October, 1939, 322-332.

Bennett, G. "The Development of Political Organizations in Kenya," *Political Studies,* V, no. 2 (June, 1957), 119-122.

Benson, T. G. "The Jeanes School and the Education of the East African Native," *Journal of the Royal African Society,* XXV, no. 141 (October, 1936), 418-431.

Bewes, Canon. "Missionary on Mau Mau," *Times Educational Supplement,* no. 1972 (February 13, 1953), 134.

Bigelow, Karl. "Some Major Educational Problems in Africa South of the Sahara: A Critical Summary," *Journal of Negro Education,* XXX, no. 3, (Summer, 1961), 343-357.

Binns, A. L. "Education of Africans in East and Central Africa," *Colonial Review,* VII (December, 1952), 232-235.

Callaway, Archibald. "Unemployment Among African School Leavers," *Journal of Modern African Studies,* I, no. 3 (September, 1963), 351-372.

Carlin, M. M. "The Midas Touch: Some Observations on the Como Report," *Makerere Journal,* March, 1964, 45-52.

Carpenter, George Wayland. "African Education and the Christian Missions," *Phi Delta Kappan,* XLI, no. 4 (January, 1960), 191-195.

"Christian Mission Educational Policy in East Africa," *Oversea Education,* XII, no. 2 (January, 1941), 84-86.

"Church and State," *Reporter,* III, no. 100 (February 14, 1964), 33.

"Church Schools," *Reporter,* III, no. 94 (December 14, 1963), 41.

Creighton, T. R. M. "Education and Society in East Africa," *Oversea Quarterly,* I (December, 1958), 104-106.

Currie, Sir James and others. "Indirect Rule in Africa and its Bearing on Educational Development," *Oversea Education,* IV, no. 2 (January, 1933), 82-84.

Denoon, Donald, and Kuper, Adam. "The New Historiography in Dar es Salaam." *African Affairs,* LXIX, no. 277 (October, 1970), 329-349.

"Education and Colonial Development," *Nature,* CLXI, no. 4103 (June 19, 1948), 947-950.

Elvin, Lionel. "Education and Community Development: Some Recent Trends in Africa," *Fundamental and Adult Education,* IX, no. 2 (April, 1957), 59-62.

Evans, P. C. C. "American Teachers for East Africa," *Comparative Education Review,* VI (June, 1962), 69-77.

_____. "Western Education and Rural Productivity in Tropical Africa," *Africa,* XXXII, no. 4 (October, 1962), 313-323.

Frankel, S. H. "The Tyranny of Economic Paternalism in Africa," *Optima,* (suppl.) X, no. 4 (December, 1960).

Fullani, Bin Fullani. "Religion and Common Life: A Problem in East African Missions," *International Review of Missions,* VIII, 155-172.

Gichuru, James. "Making Kenya a Good Bet for the Investor," *East African Standard,* December 12, 1962, p. 8.

Harbison, Frederick W. "Education for Development," *Scientific American,* CCIX, no. 3 (September, 1963), 140-147.

Hunter, Guy. "Emerging Africans," *Adult Education,* XXII, no. 2 (Autumn, 1959), 101-107.

International Bank for Reconstruction and Development. *The Economic Development of Kenya.* As reviewed by J. S. Skinner in the *Journal of Modern African Studies,* III, no. 4 (December, 1963), 551-552.

"Jobs for 50,000," *Reporter,* III, no. 100 (February 14, 1964), 25, 26.

Khamisi, F. J. "The East African Political Scene: The African Viewpoint," *African Affairs,* XLV, no. 180 (July, 1946), 139-141.

Kilson, Martin L. "Land and the Kikuyu: A Study of the Relationship Between Land and Kikuyu Political Movements," *Journal of Negro History,* XL, no. 2 (April, 1955), 103-153.

Kimp, Kenneth J. "Africa and the Southern States of the U.S.A.: Notes on J. H. Oldham and American Negro Education for Africans," *Journal of African History,* X, no. 4 (1969), 659-677.

Kioni, S. J. "Religion in the Schools," K.N.U.T. Newsletter, *East African Standard,* III, no. 95.

——————. "K.N.U.T. Newsletter," *Reporter,* III, no. 88 (November 2, 1963), 26.

——————. "K.N.U.T. Newsletter," *Reporter,* III, no. 97 (January 4, 1964), p. 15.

Latham, G. C. "Indirect Rule and Education in East Africa," *Africa,* VII, no. 4 (October, 1934), 423-430.

Lewis, L. J. "Education and Political Independence in Africa," *Comparative Education Review,* V, no. 1 (June, 1961), 39-49.

Maleche, Albert. "Rural Transformation?" *Africa Today,* XIV, no. 2 (1967), 29-31.

Mason, Edwin S. "The Planning of Development," *Scientific American,* CCIX, no. 3 (September, 1963), 235-236.

Maxwell, Robert. "Teaching Agriculture in Secondary Schools," *East Africa Journal* (June, 1965), 27-28.

Mazrui, Ali. "European Exploration and Africa's Self-Discovery," *Journal of Modern African Studies,* VII, no. 4 (1969), 661-676.

Mwendwa, Kyale. "Kenya Institute of Education," *Teacher Education Bulletin.* Nairobi: Equatorial Publishers, 1967.

Nye, Joseph S., Jr. "East African Economic Integration," *The Journal of Modern African Studies,* I, no. 4 (December, 1963), 475-502.

"Objectives in the Education of Colonial Peoples," *Nature,* CLXIV, no. 4169 (September 24, 1949), 526-527.

Otiende, J. "The Clamour for Learning," *East African Standard* (December 12, 1963), p. 12.

Perham, Margery. "The Psychology of African Nationalism," *Optima,* X, no. 1 (March, 1960), 27-36.

Ranger, Terence. "African Attempts to Control Education in East and Central Africa 1900-1939." *Past and Present,* XXXII (December, 1965), 57-85.

Read, Margaret H. "Education in Africa: Its Pattern and Role in Social Change," *The Annals of the American Academy of Political Science,* CCXCVIII (March, 1955), 170-179.

"Report of the Commission on Higher Education in East Africa: A Summary of its Conclusions," *Oversea Education,* IX, no. 2 (March, 1938), 57-64.

Rosberg, Carl G., Jr. "Independent Kenya: Problems and Prospects," *Africa Report,* VIII, no. 11 (December, 1963), 3-7.

——————, and Segal, Aaron. "An East African Federation," *International Conciliation,* No. 543, New York, Carnegie Endowment for International Peace. May 1963.

Scanlon, David G. "The Bush School," *Phi Delta Kappan,* XLI, no. 4 (January, 1960), 148-150.

——————. "Education and Nationalism in Kenya and the Gold Coast," *Teachers College Record,* LVI, no. 6 (March, 1955), 38-49.

"Six-Year Plan," *Reporter,* III, no. 101 (February 24, 1964), p. 29.

United Nations Economic Commission for Africa. *Economic Bulletin for Africa,* II, no. 2 (June, 1962).

University of London, Institute of Education. "Education in Africa: A Select Bibliography," Part I, *Education Libraries Bulletin,* Supplement Five, 1962. Compiled by Margaret Couch.

Vaizey, John. "Comparative Notes on Economic Growth and Social Change in Education," *Comparative Education Review,* V, no. 1 (June, 1961), 7-12.

Wallbank, T. W. "British Colonial Policy and Native Education in Kenya," *Journal of Negro Education,* VII, no. 4 (October, 1938), 521-532.

Ward, R. E. F. "The East African Political Scene: The European Point of View," *African Affairs,* XLV, no. 180 (July, 1946), 136-139.

——————. "Educational Progress in Britain's Dependencies Since 1945." *Educational Forum,* XXII, no. 4, Part 1 (May, 1958), 445-446.

——————. "The Beecher Report on African Education in Kenya," *Oversea Education,* XXIV, no. 4 (January, 1953), 13-19.

Weatherhead, H. W. "The Educational Value of Industrial Work as Illustrated in King's School, Budo, Uganda," *International Review of Missions,* III, 343-348.

Wingard, P. C. "East Africa," *Review of Educational Research,* XXXII, no. 3, (June, 1962), 294-297.

Wrong, Margaret. "The Educational Approach to the Family," *Oversea Education,* XII, no. 2 (January, 1941), 47-51.

Unpublished Materials

Atlantic Institute. "Education in Under-Developed Countries: Summary of Documents," Prepared for the Seminar on Aid to Education in Less Developed Countries. Bellagio, Italy, July 11-19, 1962. (Mimeographed.)

Berman, Edward. "Education in Africa and America: A History of the Phelps-Stokes Fund 1911-1945." Unpublished Ph.D. dissertation, Teachers College, Columbia University, 1969.

Bigelow, Karl. "Implications of the Report of the Conference on the Development of Higher Education in Africa: For the Provision for Africans of Study Opportunities Overseas." New York: Teachers College, 1962. (Mimeographed.)

Brownstein, Lewis. "Mass Education in a Developing Society: The Case of the Kenya Preliminary Examination Candidate." Unpublished Ph.D. dissertation, John Hopkins University, 1969.

——————. "Preliminary Results of a Survey of 1964 K.P.E. Candidates in Embu, Kitui, Kericho and Nyanza." Institute for Development Studies, University College, Nairobi, discussion paper 58, November, 1969. (Mimeographed.)

Campbell, L. J., headmaster of Alliance High School, Kikuyu, Kenya. Letter to author dated December 16, 1963.

Curle, Adam. "The Role of Education in Developing Societies," Inaugural Lecture delivered at the University College of Ghana, February 15, 1961. (Mimeographed.)

Dain, F. R. Executive Secretary to the Christian Churches Educational Association. Letter to author dated December 31, 1963.

Doro, Marion Elizabeth. "Kenya: A Case Study of the Development of Western Political Institutions in a Plural Society." Unpublished Ph.D. dissertation, University of Pennsylvania, 1959. (Typewritten.)

Fields, Ralph R. "Semi-Annual Report from Teachers College, Columbia University, to the Agency for International Development on the Teachers For East Africa Projects." Covering the Progress made under ICAa-1911 from April 25, 1961 to October 31, 1961. (Also reports covering November 1, 1961 to May 31, 1962 and June 1, 1962 to December 15, 1962).

Franklin, Donald B. "The Kikuyu Independent Schools: A Study of the Response and the Colonial Government in Kenya." Unpublished M.A. thesis, Teachers College, Columbia University, 1967.

Heyman, Richard. "The Role of the Carnegie Corporation in African Education 1925-1960." Ed.D. dissertation, Teachers College, Columbia University, 1969.

Hunter, Guy. "High-Level Manpower in East Africa: Preliminary Assessment." 2nd draft. (Consultant, Professor F. H. Harbison, Princeton University.) Unpublished manuscript, August, 1962.

Kampala, Uganda, East African Institute of Social Research, Makerere College. *Conference,* January, 1962. (Typewritten.)

Kimp, Kenneth J. "The Politics of Agricultural Education for Africans in Kenya." A paper presented at the Annual Conference of the Historical Association of Kenya, August, 1969. (Mimeographed.)

Lewis, Arthur J., and Lieb, L. V. (eds.). "A Report of the Conference on Institutes of Education," January 27-30, 1964, Mombasa, Kenya, East Africa. (Mimeographed.)

――――――. "Semi-Annual Report from Teachers College, Columbia University to the Agency for International Development on the Teachers For East Africa Project." Covering the Progress made under ICAa-1911 from December 16, 1962-June 30, 1963.

Moris, Jon. "Education and Training of the Farmer." Paper presented at the Conference on Education, Employment and Rural Development, Kericho, Kenya, September, 1966.

Odhiambo, Thomas R. and Okumo, Washington A. J. "Policies and Objectives of Education in Independent Kenya." A memorandum submitted to the Kenya Education Commission, March, 1964.

Othieno, N. Antipa. "An Outline of History of Education in East Africa." Unpublished Doctor of Education project report, Teachers College, Columbia University, 1963.

"Report of a Conference on the University of East Africa." Villa Serbelloni, Bellagio, Italy. October 21-25, 1963. (Mimeographed.)

Williams, Edwin. "A Historiographical Review of the Writings of Terence Ranger of East Central and South Africa." January, 1969. (Mimeographed.)

Index

academic education, 96; vs. vocational education, 11, 20-21, 24, 42, 76, 98, 99, 100-101
academic reform, 48, 65, 69, 88, 95-98. *See also* Africanization of education; curriculum development
Addis Ababa Conference, 68-69, 70; Plan(s), 70, 72; Report of, 68-69, 71, 90
adult education, 47, 65, 69, 70, 87, 89, 99, 100-101. *See also* community development
Advisory Committee on Education, 19; Memorandum of (1925), 19-20, 24, 28, 42, 46
African District Councils, 57
African ministers of education, permanent conference of, 70
Africanization of education, 46, 64, 65, 66, 69, 72, 74, 94, 96
agricultural training, 23, 46, 47, 66, 69, 73, 75, 97-99; African opposition to, 20, 66, 98-99; early, by missions, 9
Agency for International Development (AID), 97
"airlifts" to U.S., 64, 86
Alliance High School, 21, 24, 63
Anderson, C. Arnold, 74
Anglican Church Missionary Society (CMS), 8-9, 10, 27
Ashby Report (1960), 59, 65, 69
Asquith Commission (1943), 31
African Liaison Committee of the American Council on Education, 65

Bagamoyo, Catholic mission at, 9
Beecher, L.J., 33, 48, 64

Beecher Committee, 33; Report of, 41-44, 45, 46, 49, 62, 63, 66, 68, 79
Binns, A.L., 45-47, 48
Binns Report, 45-47; comparison with Beecher Report, 45, 46
"bonding," 93
"bush schools," 2, 21

Cambridge Conference, 45, 47-49
Cambridge Examinations, 96
Cambridge Overseas School Certificate, 96
Cambridge Syndicate, 96, 97
Cameron, Sir Donald, 25
Campbell, L.J., 63
Certificate of Primary Education, 95
Chavakali, *Harambee* day school at, 97
Church of Scotland, 10, 12
citizenship, education for, 65
Colonial Development and Welfare Act of 1940, 49; of 1945, 31, 32, 49
community development, 19-20, 25, 46, 69, 98-100; Special Rural Development Program for, 100
Como Conference (1963), 67-68
Conference of African States on the Development of Education in Africa. *See* Addis Ababa Conference
Conference on Education, Employment and Rural Development. *See* Kericho Conference
cooperation between missionaries and Government, for education, 17-22, 30, 42, 48; to further colonialism, 10-11
cultural nationalism. *See* nationalism, cultural